YOU CAN BE brave

TOMORROW'S
DREAM
BEGINS
WITH
TODAY'S
COURAGE

Also by Max Lucado

INSPIRATIONAL

3:16
A Gentle Thunder
A Love Worth Giving
And the Angels Were Silent
Anxious for Nothing
Because of Bethlehem
Before Amen
Come Thirsty
Cure for the Common Life
Facing Your Giants
Fearless
Glory Days
God Came Near
God Never Gives Up on You
Grace
Great Day Every Day
He Chose the Nails
He Still Moves Stones
Help Is Here
How Happiness Happens
In the Eye of the Storm
In the Grip of Grace
It's Not About Me333333
Just Like Jesus
Max on Life
More to Your Story
Next Door Savior
No Wonder They Call Him the Savior
On the Anvil
Outlive Your Life
Six Hours One Friday
Tame Your Thoughts
The Applause of Heaven
The Great House of God
Traveling Light
Unshakable Hope
What Happens Next
When Christ Comes
When God Whispers Your Name
You Are Never Alone
You'll Get Through This
You Were Made for This Moment

COMPILATIONS

Begin Again
In the Footsteps of the Savior
Jesus
Never Give Up
Start with Prayer
They Walked with God

FICTION

Christmas Stories
Miracle at the Higher Grounds Café
The Christmas Candle

BIBLES (GENERAL EDITOR)

The Lucado Encouraging Word Bible
Children's Daily Devotional Bible
Grace for the Moment Daily Bible
The Lucado Life Lessons Study Bible

CHILDREN'S BOOKS

A Max Lucado Children's Treasury
Bedtime Prayers for Little Ones
God Bless This Child
Grace for the Moment: 365 Devotions for Kids
Hermie, a Common Caterpillar
I'm Not a Scaredy Cat
Itsy Bitsy Christmas
Just in Case You Ever Wonder
Just in Case You Ever Feel Alone
Lucado Treasury of Bedtime Prayers
One Hand, Two Hands
Thank You, God, for Blessing Me
Thank You, God, for Loving Me
The Crippled Lamb
The Oak Inside the Acorn
Where'd My Giggle Go?

YOUNG ADULT BOOKS

3:16
Make Every Day Count
Wild Grace
You Were Made to Make a Difference
Anxious for Nothing (Young Readers Edition)
One God, One Plan, One Life
Unshakable Hope Promise Book
You Can Count on God

GIFT BOOKS

Calm Moments for Anxious Days
Everyday Blessings
God Is with You Every Day
God Thinks You're Wonderful
God Will Carry You Through
God Will Help You
Grace for the Moment
Grace for the Moment Family Devotional
Grace for the Moment for Moms
Grace for the Moment: Morning and Evening
Grace Happens Here
Happy Today
Let the Journey Begin
Praying the Promises
Safe in the Shepherd's Arms
Trade Your Cares for Calm
You Can Count on God
You Changed My Life

YOU CAN BE brave

TOMORROW'S **DREAM BEGINS** WITH TODAY'S **COURAGE**

MAX LUCADO

THOMAS NELSON
Since 1798

You Can Be Brave

This book was adapted from *Fearless*, © 2009 by Max Lucado.

Published by Thomas Nelson, 501 Nelson Place, Nashville, TN 37214, USA. Thomas Nelson is a registered trademark of HarperCollins Christian Publishing, Inc.

Thomas Nelson titles may be purchased in bulk for educational, business, fundraising, or sales promotional use. For information, please email SpecialMarkets@ThomasNelson.com.

Cover Design: Jamie DeBruyn
Interior Design: Lori Lynch
Cover Image: istock

ISBN 978-1-4003-4288-4 (audiobook)
ISBN 978-1-4003-4285-3 (eBook)
ISBN 978-1-4003-4282-2 (hardcover)

HarperCollins Publishers, Macken House, 39/40 Mayor Street Upper, Dublin 1, D01 C9W8, Ireland (https://www.harpercollins.com)

Library of Congress Cataloging-in-Publication Data on File

Printed in the United States of America

26 27 28 29 30 LBC 5 4 3 2 1

Contents

1

Why Are You Afraid?

Why are you fearful, O you of little faith?

—Matthew 8:26

You would have liked my brother. Everyone did. Dee made friends the way bakers make bread: daily, easily, warmly. Handshake—big and eager; laughter—contagious and volcanic. He permitted no stranger to remain one for long. I, the shy younger brother, relied on him to make introductions for us both. When a family moved onto the street or a newcomer walked onto the playground, Dee was the ambassador.

But in his mid-teen years, he made one acquaintance he should have avoided—a bootlegger who sold beer to underage drinkers. Alcohol made a play for us both, but although it entwined me, it enchained him. Over the next four decades my brother drank away health, relationships, jobs, money, and all but the last two years of his life.

Who can say why resolve sometimes wins and sometimes

loses, but at the age of fifty-four my brother discovered an aquifer of willpower, drilled deep, and enjoyed a season of sobriety. He emptied his bottles, stabilized his marriage, reached out to his children, and exchanged the liquor store for the local AA. But the hard living had taken its toll.

On a January night during the week I began writing this book, he told Donna, his wife, that he couldn't breathe well. He already had a doctor's appointment for a related concern, so he decided to try to sleep. Little success. He awoke at 4:00 A.M. with chest pains severe enough to warrant a visit to the emergency room. The rescue team loaded Dee onto the gurney and told Donna to meet them at the hospital. My brother waved weakly and smiled bravely and told Donna not to worry, but by the time she and one of Dee's sons reached the hospital, he was gone.

The attending physician told them the news and invited them to step into the room where Dee's body lay. Holding each other, they walked through the doors and saw his final message. His hand was resting on the top of his thigh with the two center fingers folded in and the thumb extended, the universal sign-language symbol for "I love you."

I've tried to envision the final moments of my brother's earthly life: racing down a Texas highway in an ambulance through an inky night, paramedics buzzing around him, his heart weakening within him. Struggling for each breath, at some point he realized only a few remained. But rather than panic, he quarried some courage.

Perhaps you could use some. An ambulance isn't the only ride that demands valor. You may not be down to your final heartbeat, but you may be down to your last paycheck, solution, or thimble of faith. Each sunrise seems to bring fresh reasons for fear.

They're talking layoffs at work, slowdowns in the economy, flare-ups in the Middle East, turnovers at headquarters, downturns in the housing market, upswings in global warming, breakouts of terrorist cells. Some demented dictator is collecting nuclear warheads the way others collect fine wines. A strain of flu is crossing our country. News programs disgorge enough hand-wringing information to warrant an advisory: "Caution: This news report is best viewed in the confines of an underground vault in Iceland."

We fear being sued, finishing last, going broke; we fear the mole on the back, the new kid on the block, the sound of the clock as it ticks us closer to the grave. We sophisticate investment plans, create elaborate security systems, and legislate stronger military, yet we depend on mood-altering drugs more than any other generation in history. Moreover, I've heard it said that ordinary children today are more fearful than psychiatric patients were in the 1950s.

Fear, it seems, has taken a hundred-year lease on the building next door and set up shop. Oversize and rude, fear is unwilling to share the heart with happiness. Can one be happy and afraid at the same time? Clear-thinking and afraid?

Confident and afraid? Merciful and afraid? No. For all the noise fear makes and the room it takes, fear does little good.

Fear never wrote a symphony or poem, negotiated a peace treaty, or cured a disease. Fear never pulled a family out of poverty or a country out of bigotry. Fear never saved a marriage or a business. Courage did that. Faith did that. Brave people who refused to consult or cower to their timidities did that. But fear itself? Fear herds us into a prison and slams the doors.

Wouldn't it be great to walk out?

Imagine your life wholly untouched by angst. What if faith, not fear, was your default reaction to threats? Envision a day, just one day, absent the dread of failure, rejection, and calamity. Can you imagine a life with no fear? This is the possibility behind Jesus' question. "Why are you afraid?" he asks (Matt. 8:26 NCV).

At first blush we wonder whether Jesus is serious. He may be kidding. Teasing. Pulling a quick one. Kind of like one swimmer asking another, "Why are you wet?" But Jesus doesn't smile. He's dead earnest. So are the men to whom he asks the question. A storm has turned their Galilean dinner cruise into a white-knuckled plunge.

Here is how Matthew remembered the trip: "Jesus got into a boat, and his followers went with him. A great storm arose on the lake so that waves covered the boat" (Matt. 8:23–24 NCV).

Peter and John, seasoned sailors, struggle to keep down the sail. Matthew, confirmed landlubber, struggles to keep down his breakfast. The storm is not what the tax collector bargained for. Do you sense his surprise in the way he links his two sentences? "Jesus got into a boat, and his followers went with him. A great storm arose on the lake."

Wouldn't you hope for a more chipper second sentence, a happier consequence of obedience? "Jesus got into a boat. His followers went with him, and suddenly a great rainbow arched in the sky, a flock of doves hovered in happy formation, a sea of glass mirrored their mast." Don't Christ-followers enjoy a calendar full of Caribbean cruises? No. This story sends the not-so-subtle and not-too-popular reminder: Getting on board with Christ can mean getting soaked with Christ. Disciples can expect rough seas and stout winds. "In the world you will [not *might, may*, or *could*] have tribulation" (John 16:33, brackets mine).

Christ-followers contract pneumonia, bury children, and battle addictions, and, as a result, face fears. It's not the absence of storms that sets us apart. It's whom we discover in the storm: an unstirred Christ.

"Jesus was sleeping" (Matt. 8:24 NCV).

Now there's a scene. The disciples scream; Jesus dreams. Thunder roars; Jesus snores. He doesn't doze, catnap, or rest. He slumbers. Could you sleep at a time like this? Could you snooze during a roller coaster loop-the-loop? In a wind tunnel? At a kettledrum concert? Jesus sleeps through all three at once!

Mark's gospel adds two curious details: "[Jesus] was in the

stern, asleep on a pillow" (Mark 4:38). In the stern, on a pillow. Why the first? Whence came the second?

First-century fishermen used large, heavy seine nets for their work. They stored the nets in a nook that was built into the stern for this purpose. Sleeping *on* the stern deck was impractical. It provided no space or protection. The small compartment beneath the stern, however, provided both. It was the most enclosed and only protected part of the boat. Christ, a bit dozy from the day's activities, crawled beneath the deck to get some sleep.

He rested his head, not on a fluffy feather pillow, but on a leather sandbag. A ballast bag. Mediterranean fishermen still use them. They weigh about a hundred pounds and are used to ballast, or stabilize, the boat.[1] Did Jesus take the pillow to the stern so he could sleep, or sleep so soundly that someone rustled him up the pillow? We don't know. But this much we do know. This was a premeditated slumber. He didn't accidentally nod off. In full knowledge of the coming storm, Jesus decided it was siesta time, so he crawled into the corner, put his head on the pillow, and drifted into dreamland.

His snooze troubles the disciples. Matthew and Mark record their responses as three staccato Greek pronouncements and one question.

The pronouncements: "Lord! Save! Dying!" (Matt. 8:25).

The question: "Teacher, do You not care that we are perishing?" (Mark 4:38).

They do not ask about Jesus' strength: "Can you still the storm?" His knowledge: "Are you aware of the storm?" Or his know-how: "Do you have any experience with storms?" Rather, they raise doubts about Jesus' character: "Do you not care . . ."

Fear does this. Fear corrodes our confidence in God's goodness. We begin to wonder if love lives in heaven. If God can sleep in our storms, if his eyes stay shut when our eyes grow wide, if he permits storms after we get on his boat, does he care? Fear unleashes a swarm of doubts, anger-stirring doubts.

And it turns us into control freaks. "Do something about the storm!" is the implicit demand of the question. "Fix it or . . . or . . . or else!" Fear, at its center, is a perceived loss of control. When life spins wildly, we grab for a component of life we can manage: our diet, the tidiness of a house, the armrest of a plane, or, in many cases, people. The more insecure we feel, the meaner we become. We growl and bare our fangs. Why? Because we are bad? In part. But also because we feel cornered.

Fear also deadens our recall. The disciples had reason to trust Jesus. By now they'd seen him "healing all kinds of sickness and all kinds of disease among the people" (Matt. 4:23). Peter saw his sick mother-in-law recover (Matt. 8:14–15), and they all saw demons scatter like bats out of a cave. "He cast out the spirits with a word, and healed all who were sick" (Matt. 8:16).

Shouldn't someone mention Jesus' track record or review his résumé? Do they remember the accomplishments of Christ? They may not. Fear creates a form of spiritual amnesia. It dulls our miracle memory. It makes us forget what Jesus has done and how good God is.

And fear feels dreadful. It sucks the life out of the soul, curls us into an embryonic state, and drains us dry of contentment. When fear shapes our lives, safety becomes our god. When safety becomes our god, we worship the risk-free life. Can the safety lover do anything great? Can the risk-averse accomplish noble deeds? For God? For others? No. The fear-filled cannot love deeply. Love is risky. They cannot give to the poor. Benevolence has no guarantee of return. The fear-filled cannot dream wildly. What if their dreams sputter and fall from the sky? The worship of safety emasculates greatness. No wonder Jesus wages such a war against fear.

His most common command emerges from the "fear not" genre. The Gospels list some 125 Christ-issued imperatives. Of these, 21 urge us to "not be afraid" or "not fear" or "have courage" or "take heart" or "be of good cheer." The second most common of his commands—to love God and neighbor—appears on only 8 occasions. If quantity is any indicator, Jesus takes our fears seriously. The one statement he made more than any other was this: Don't be afraid.

> So don't be afraid. You are worth much more than many sparrows. (Matt. 10:31 NCV)

> Don't be afraid. Just believe, and your daughter will be well. (Luke 8:50 NCV)

> Take courage. I am here! (Matt. 14:27 NLT)
>
> Do not fear those who kill the body but cannot kill the soul. (Matt. 10:28)
>
> Do not fear, little flock, for it is your Father's good pleasure to give you the kingdom. (Luke 12:32)
>
> Don't let your hearts be troubled. Trust in God, and trust also in me. (John 14:1 NLT)
>
> You will hear of wars and rumors of wars, but see to it that you are not alarmed. (Matt. 24:6 NIV)

Jesus doesn't want you to live in a state of fear. Nor do you. You've never made statements like these:

- My phobias put such a spring in my step.
- Thank God for my pessimism. I've been such a better person since I lost hope.
- My doctor says if I don't begin fretting, I will lose my health.

We've learned the high cost of fear.

Jesus' question is a good one. He lifts his head from the pillow, steps out from the stern into the storm, and asks, "Why are you fearful, O you of little faith?" (Matt. 8:26).

To be clear, fear serves a healthy function. A dose of fright can keep a child from running across a busy road or an adult from smoking a pack of cigarettes. Fear is the appropriate reaction to a burning building or growling dog. Fear itself is not a sin. But it can lead to sin.

If we medicate fear with angry outbursts, drinking binges, sullen withdrawals, self-starvation, or viselike control, we exclude God from the solution and exacerbate the problem. We subject ourselves to a position of fear, allowing anxiety to dominate and define our lives. Joy-sapping worries. Day-numbing dread. Repeated bouts of insecurity that petrify and paralyze us. Hysteria is not from God. "For God has not given us a spirit of fear" (2 Tim. 1:7).

Fear may fill our world, but it doesn't have to fill our hearts. It will always knock on the door. Just don't invite it in for dinner, and for heaven's sake don't offer it a bed for the night. Let's embolden our hearts with a select number of Jesus' "do not fear" statements. The promise of Christ and the contention of this book are simple: We can fear less tomorrow than we do today. We can be brave.

When I was six years old, my dad let me stay up late with the rest of the family and watch the movie *The Wolf Man*. Boy, did he regret that decision. The film left me convinced that a wolf man spent each night prowling our den, awaiting his preferred meal of first-grade, redheaded, freckle-salted boy. My fear proved problematic. To reach the kitchen from my bedroom, I had to pass perilously close to his claws and fangs, something I was loath to do. More than once I retreated to my father's bedroom and awoke him. Like Jesus in the boat, Dad was sound asleep in the storm. *How can a person sleep at a time like this?*

Opening a sleepy eye, he would ask, "Now, why are you afraid?" And I would remind him of the monster. "Oh yes, the Wolf Man," he'd grumble. He would then climb out of bed, arm himself with superhuman courage, escort me through the valley of the shadow of death, and pour me a glass of milk. I would look at him with awe and wonder. *What kind of man is this?*

Might it be that God views our storms the way my father viewed my wolf man angst? "Jesus got up and gave a command to the wind and the waves, and it became completely calm" (Matt. 8:26 NCV).

He handles the great quaking with a great calming. The sea becomes as still as a frozen lake, and the disciples are left wondering, "What kind of man is this? Even the winds and the waves obey him!" (v. 27 NCV).

What kind of man, indeed. Turning typhoon time into nap time. Silencing waves with one word. And equipping a dying man with sufficient courage to send a final love message to his family. Way to go, Dee. You faced your share of stormy moments in life, but in the end you didn't go under.

Here's a prayer that we won't either.

2

God's Ticked Off at Me

Take courage, son; your sins are forgiven.

—Matthew 9:2 NASB

Noble Doss dropped the ball. One ball. One pass. One mistake. In 1941 he let one fall. And it's haunted him ever since. "I cost us a national championship," he says.

The University of Texas football team was ranked number one in the nation. Hoping for an undefeated season and a berth in the Rose Bowl, they played conference rival Baylor University. With a 7–0 lead in the third quarter, the Longhorn quarterback launched a deep pass to a wide-open Doss.

"The only thing I had between me and the goal," he recalls, "was twenty yards of grass."

The throw was on target. Longhorn fans rose to their feet. The sure-handed Doss spotted the ball and reached out, but it slipped through.

Baylor rallied and tied the score with seconds to play.

Texas lost their top ranking and, consequently, their chance at the Rose Bowl.

"I think about that play every day," Doss admits.

Not that he lacks other memories. Happily married for more than six decades. A father. Grandfather. He served in the navy during World War II. He appeared on the cover of *Life* magazine with his Texas teammates. He intercepted seventeen passes during his collegiate career, a university record. He won two NFL titles with the Philadelphia Eagles. The Texas High School Football Hall of Fame and the Longhorn Hall of Honor include his name.

Most fans remember the plays Doss made and the passes he caught. Doss remembers the one he missed.[1]

Memories of dropped passes fade slowly. They stir a lonely fear, a fear that we have disappointed people, that we have let down the team, that we've come up short. A fear that, when needed, we didn't do our part, that others suffered from our fumbles and bumbles. Of course, some of us would gladly swap our blunders for Doss's. If only we'd merely dropped a pass. If only we'd merely disappointed a football squad.

I converse often with a fellow who, by his own admission, wasted the first half of his life. Blessed with more talent than common sense, he made enemies and money at breakneck speed. Now he's the stuff of which sad country songs are written. Ruined marriage. Angry kids. His liver functions as if it's been soaked in vodka. (It has.)

When we talk, his eyes dart back and forth like a man hearing footsteps. His past pursues him like a posse. Our conversations return to the same orbit: "Can God ever forgive me?" "He gave me a wife; I blew it. He gave me kids; I blew it." I try to tell him, "Yes, you failed, but you aren't a failure. God came for people like us." He absorbs my words the way the desert absorbs a downpour. But by the next time I see him, he needs to hear them again. The parched soil of fear needs steady rain.

"God's well of grace must have a bottom to it," we reason. "A person can request forgiveness only so many times," contends our common sense. "Cash in too many mercy checks, and sooner or later one is going to bounce!" The devil loves this line of logic. If he can convince us that God's grace has limited funds, we'll draw the logical conclusion. The account is empty. God has locked the door to his throne room. Pound all you want; pray all you want. No access to God.

"No access to God" unleashes a beehive of concerns. We are orphans, unprotected and exposed. Heaven, if there is such a place, has been removed from the itinerary. Vulnerable in this life and doomed in the next. The fear of disappointing God has teeth.

But we can be brave. In Christ's first reference to fear, he does some serious defanging. "Take courage, son; your sins are forgiven" (Matt. 9:2 NASB). Note how Jesus places *courage* and *forgiven sins* in the same sentence. Might bravery begin when the problem of sin is solved? Let's see.

Jesus spoke these words to a person who could not move. "A paralytic lying on a bed . . . " (v. 2 NASB). The disabled man couldn't walk the dog or jog the neighborhood. But he did have four friends, and his friends had a hunch. When they got wind that Jesus was a guest in their town, they loaded their companion onto a mat and went to see the teacher. An audience with Christ might bode well for their buddy.

A standing-room-only crowd packed the residence where Jesus spoke. People sat in windows, crowded in doorways. You'd have thought God himself was making the Capernaum appearance. Being the sort of fellows who don't give up easily, the friends concocted a plan. "When they weren't able to get in because of the crowd, they removed part of the roof and lowered the paraplegic on his stretcher" (Mark 2:4 MSG).

Risky strategy. Most homeowners don't like to have their roofs disassembled. Most paraplegics aren't fond of a one-way bungee drop through a ceiling cavity. And most teachers don't appreciate a spectacle in the midst of their lesson. We don't know the reaction of the homeowner or the man on the mat. But we know that Jesus didn't object. Matthew all but paints a smile on his face. Christ issued a blessing no one expected: "Take courage, son; your sins are forgiven." Wouldn't we anticipate different words? "Take courage. Your legs are healed." "Your paralysis is over." "Sign up for the Boston Marathon."

The man had limbs as sturdy as spaghetti, yet Jesus offered mercy, not muscles. What was he thinking? Simple. He was thinking about our deepest problem: sin. He was considering our deepest fear: the fear of failing God. Before Jesus healed the body (which he did), he treated the soul. "Take courage, son; your sins are forgiven."

To sin is to disregard God, ignore his teachings, deny his blessings. Sin is "God-less" living, centering life on the center letter of the word *sIn*. The sinner's life is me-focused, not God-focused.

We are convinced that God must hate our evil tendencies. We sure do. We despise our lustful thoughts, harsh judgments, and selfish deeds. If our sin nauseates us, how much more must it revolt a holy God! We draw a practical conclusion: God is irreparably ticked off at us.

The prophet Isaiah says that sin has left us as lost and confused as stray sheep. "All we like sheep have gone astray; we have turned, every one, to his own way" (Isa. 53:6). If the prophet had known my dog, he might have written, "All we like Molly have gone astray . . ."

For such a sweet dog, she has a stubborn, defiant streak. Once her nose gets wind of a neighbor's grilling steak or uncovered trash, no cajoling or commands can control her. You don't want to know how many times this minister has chased his dog down the street, tossing un-minister-like warnings at his pet. She "sins," living as if her master doesn't exist. She is known to wander.

Last week we thought she'd wandered away for good. We posted her picture on bulletin boards, drove through the neighborhood calling her name. Finally, after a day of futility, I went to the animal shelter. I described Molly to the animal shelter director. She wished me luck and pointed toward a barrack-shaped building whose door bore the sign Stray Dogs.

Two terriers, according to a note on the gate, were found on a remote highway. Someone found an aging poodle in an alley. I thought I'd found her when I spotted a golden retriever with salty hair. But it wasn't Molly. It was a he with eyes so brown and lonely they nearly landed him a place in my back seat.

I didn't find Molly at the shelter.

I did have a crazy urge at the shelter, however. I wanted to announce Jesus' declaration: "Be of good cheer. You are lost no more!" I wanted to take the strays home with me, to unlock door after door and fill my car with barking, tail-wagging *dog*igals. I didn't do it. As much as I wanted to save the dogs, I wanted to stay married even more.

But I did have the urge, and the urge helps me understand why Jesus made forgiveness his first fearless announcement. Yes, we have disappointed God. But, no, God has not abandoned us.

> [We are] delivered . . . from the power of darkness and conveyed . . . into the kingdom of the Son. (Col. 1:13)

> These things I have written to you who believe in the name of the Son of God, that you may know that you have eternal life. (1 John 5:13)

Jesus loves us too much to leave us in doubt about his grace. His "perfect love expels all fear" (1 John 4:18 NLT). If God loved with an imperfect love, we would have high cause to worry. Imperfect love keeps a list of sins and consults it often. God keeps no list of our wrongs. His love casts out fear because he casts out our sin!

Tether your heart to this promise and tighten the knot. Remember the words of John's epistle: "If our heart condemns us, God is greater than our heart, and knows all things" (1 John 3:20). When you feel unforgiven, evict the feelings. Emotions don't get a vote. Go back to Scripture. God's Word holds rank over self-criticism and self-doubt.

As Paul told Titus, "God's readiness to give and forgive is now public. Salvation's available for everyone! . . . Tell them all this. Build up their courage" (Titus 2:11, 15 MSG). Do you know God's grace? Then you can love boldly, live robustly. You can swing from trapeze to trapeze; his safety net will break your fall.

Nothing fosters courage like a clear grasp of grace.

And nothing fosters fear like an ignorance of mercy. May I speak candidly? If you haven't accepted God's forgiveness, you are doomed to fear. Nothing can deliver you from the gnawing realization that you have disregarded your Maker and disobeyed his instruction. No pill, pep talk, psychiatrist, or possession can set the sinner's heart at ease. You may deaden the fear, but you can't remove it. Only God's grace can.

Have you accepted the forgiveness of Christ? If not, do so. "If we confess our sins, He is faithful and just to forgive us our sins and to cleanse us from all unrighteousness" (1 John 1:9). Your prayer can be as simple as this: *Dear Father, I need forgiveness. I admit that I have turned away from you. Please forgive me. I place my soul in your hands and my trust in your grace. Through Jesus I pray, amen.*

Having received God's forgiveness, live forgiven! Jesus has healed your legs, so walk. Jesus has opened the cage of the kennel, so step out. When Jesus sets you free, you are free indeed.

By the way, the case of the missing Molly? She turned up in a neighbor's backyard. Turns out she wasn't as far from home as we all feared. Neither are you.

3

Woe, Be Gone

I tell you not to worry about everyday
life—whether you have enough.

—Matthew 6:25 NLT

Worry stands in the airport security line and removes her bracelet. She's already placed her laptop in a rubberized bin and liquids in the plastic bag. Her stomach tightens as she awaits her turn to step through the body scanner that will identify her as weaponless. Worry wonders about the fungus on the floor, the skill of the screeners, and the mental health of the pilot. She hates the thought but permits it anyway: *Any day now our luck is going to run out.* She looks beyond the X-ray machine to the TSA agent, who runs a wand around the body of a grandmother. Worry starts to feel sorry for her, then decides not to. Terrorists grow old too. She worries that the grandmother is on her flight.

Worry thinks her son should wear a scarf. Today's temperature won't warm beyond freezing, and she knows he will spend the better part of his lunch hour kicking a soccer ball over the frozen grass. She knows better than to tell him to wear it. Thirteen-year-olds don't wear scarves. But her thirteen-year-old is prone to throat infections and earaches, so she shoves a wrap into his backpack next to the algebra homework that kept them both up past bedtime last night. Worry reminds him to review the assignment, gives him a kiss, and watches him run out the door to board the awaiting bus. She looks up at the gray sky and asks God if he ever air-drops relief packages to weary moms. "You have one needing some strength down here."

Worry awoke at 4:30 A.M. today, struggling with this chapter. It needs to be finished by 5:00 P.M. I pulled the pillow over my head and tried in vain to return to the blissful netherworld of sleep that knows nothing of deadlines or completion dates. But it was too late. The starter's pistol had fired. An Olympic squad of synapses was racing in my brain, stirring a wake of adrenaline. So Worry climbed out of bed, dressed, and slipped out of the house into the silent streets and drove to the office. I grumbled, first about the crowded calendar, next about my poor time management. Worry unlocked the door, turned on the computer, stared at the passage on the monitor, and smiled at the first verse: Jesus' definition of worry.

> That is why I tell you not to worry about everyday life—whether you have enough. (Matt. 6:25 NLT)

Whether you have enough. Shortfalls and depletions inhabit our trails. Not enough time, luck, credit, wisdom, intelligence. We are running out of everything, it seems, and so we worry. But worry doesn't work.

> Look at the birds. They don't plant or harvest or store food in barns, for your heavenly Father feeds them. And aren't you far more valuable to him than they are? Can all your worries add a single moment to your life? (vv. 26–27 NLT)

Fret won't fill a bird's belly with food or a flower's petal with color. Birds and flowers seem to get along just fine, and they don't take antacids. What's more, you can dedicate a decade of anxious thoughts to the brevity of life and not extend it by one minute. Worry accomplishes nothing.

Suppose I had responded differently to the uninvited wake-up call. Rather than tackle the task, suppose I had curled up in a fetal position and bemoaned my pathetic state. *The publisher expects too much! Every year another book. Every book complete with chapters. I'll never meet the deadline. Bookstores will learn of my missed deadline and will burn Lucado books in their parking lots. My wife will be humiliated, my children ostracized.*

See what happened? Legitimate concern morphed into toxic panic. I crossed a boundary line into the state of fret. No longer anticipating or preparing, I took up membership in the fraternity of Woe-Be-Me. Christ cautions us against this. Look at how one translation renders his words: "Therefore I tell you, stop being worried or anxious (perpetually uneasy, distracted) about your life" (Matt. 6:25 AMP).

Jesus doesn't condemn legitimate concern for responsibilities but rather the continuous mindset that dismisses God's presence. Destructive anxiety subtracts God from the future, faces uncertainties with no faith, tallies up the challenges of the day without entering God into the equation. Worry is the darkroom where negatives become glossy prints.

Jesus had taken his disciples on a retreat. His heart was heavied by the news of the murder of John the Baptist, so he told his disciples, "Come aside by yourselves to a deserted place and rest a while" (Mark 6:31).

But then came the hungry crowd. Droves of people—fifteen, maybe twenty, thousand individuals—followed them. A multitude of misery and sickness who brought nothing but needs. Jesus treated the people with kindness. The disciples didn't share his compassion. "That evening the disciples came to him and said, 'This is a remote place, and it's already getting late. Send the crowds away so they can go to the villages and buy food for themselves'" (Matt. 14:15 NLT).

Whoops, somebody was a bit testy. The followers typically prefaced their comments with the respectful *Lord*. Not this time. Anxiety makes tyrants out of us.

Their disrespect didn't perturb Jesus; he simply issued them an assignment: "They do not need to go away. You give them something to eat" (v. 16). I'm imagining a few shoulder shrugs and rolled eyes, the disciples huddling and tallying their supplies. Peter likely led the discussion with a bark: "Let's count the bread: one, two, three, four, five. I have five loaves. Andrew, you check me on this." He does: "One, two, three, four, five . . ."

Peter set aside the bread and inquired about the fish. Same routine, lower number. "Fish? Let me see. One, two, three . . . Change that. I counted one fish twice. Looks like the grand total of fish is two!"

The aggregate was declared. "We have here only five loaves and two fish" (v. 17). The descriptor *only* stands out. As if to say, "Our resources are hopelessly puny. There is nothing left but this wimpy lunch." The fuel needle was on empty; the clock was on the last hour; the pantry was down to crumbs.

How do you suppose Jesus felt about the basket inventory? Any chance he might have wanted them to include the rest of the possibilities? Involve all the options? Do you think he was hoping someone might count to eight?

"Well, let's see. We have five loaves, two fish, and . . . Jesus!" Jesus Christ. The same Jesus who told us:

> Ask and it will be given to you; seek and you will find; knock and the door will be opened to you. (Luke 11:9 NIV)

> Whatever you ask for in prayer, believe that you have received it, and it will be yours. (Mark 11:24 NIV)

Standing next to the disciples was the solution to their problems . . . but they didn't go to him. They stopped their count at seven and worried.

What about you? Are you counting to seven, or to eight?

Here are eight worry-stoppers to expand your tally:

1. *Pray, first.* Don't pace up and down the waiting-room floor; pray for a successful surgery. Don't bemoan the collapse of an investment; ask God to help you. Don't join the chorus of coworkers who complain about your boss; invite them to bow their heads with you and pray for him. Inoculate yourself inwardly to face your fears outwardly. "Casting all your cares [all your anxieties, all your worries, and all your concerns, once and for all] on Him" (1 Peter 5:7 AMP).

2. *Easy, now.* Slow down. "Rest in the LORD, and wait patiently for Him" (Ps. 37:7). Imitate the mother of Jesus at the wedding in Cana. "When they ran out of wine, the mother of Jesus said to Him, 'They have no wine'" (John 2:3). See how quickly you can

do the same. Assess the problem. Take it to Jesus and state it clearly.

3. *Act on it.* Become a worry-slapper. Treat frets like mosquitoes. Do you procrastinate when a bloodsucking bug lights on your skin? "I'll take care of it in a moment." Of course you don't! You give the critter the slap it deserves. Be equally decisive with anxiety. The moment a concern surfaces, deal with it. Before you diagnose that mole as cancer, have it examined. Instead of assuming you'll never get out of debt, consult an expert. Be a doer, not a stewer.

4. *Compile a worry list.* Over a period of days record your anxious thoughts. Maintain a list of all the things that trouble you. Then review them. How many of them turned into a reality? You worried that the house would burn down. Did it? That your job would be outsourced. Was it?

5. *Evaluate your worry categories.* Your list will highlight themes of worry. You'll detect recurring areas of preoccupation that may become obsessions: what people think of you, finances, global calamities, your appearance or performance. Pray specifically about them.

6. *Focus on today.* God meets daily needs daily. Not weekly or annually. He will give you what you need when it is needed. "Let us therefore boldly approach the throne of our gracious God, where we may receive mercy and in his grace find *timely* help" (Heb. 4:16 NEB).

7. *Unleash a worry army.* Share your feelings with a few loved ones. Ask them to pray with and for you.

8. *Let God be enough.* Jesus concludes his call to calmness with this challenge: "Your heavenly Father already knows all your needs. Seek the kingdom of God above all else, and live righteously, and he will give you everything you need" (Matt. 6:32–33 NLT).

Eight steps. **P**ray, first. **E**asy, now. **A**ct on it. **C**ompile a worry list. **E**valuate your worry categories. **F**ocus on today. **U**nleash a worry army. **L**et God be enough.

P-E-A-C-E-F-U-L.

(I'd better stop with that. It's nearly 5:00 P.M.)

4

My Child Is in Danger

Don't be afraid. Just believe, and
your daughter will be well.

—Luke 8:50 NCV

No one told me that newborns make nighttime noises. All night long. They gurgle; they pant. They whimper; they whine. They smack their lips and sigh. They keep Daddy awake. At least Jenna kept me awake. I wanted Denalyn to sleep. Thanks to a medication mix-up, her post-C-section rest was scant. So for our first night home with our first child, I volunteered to serve as first responder. We wrapped our eight pounds and four ounces of beauty in a soft, pink blanket, placed her in the bassinet, and set it next to my side of the bed. Denalyn fell quickly into a sound slumber. Jenna followed her mom's example. And Dad? This dad didn't know what to make of the baby noises.

When Jenna's breathing slowed, I leaned my ear onto her

mouth to see if she was alive. When her breathing hurried, I looked up "infant hyperventilation" in the family medical encyclopedia. When she burbled and panted, so did I. After a couple of hours I realized, *I have no clue how to behave!* I lifted Jenna out of her bed, carried her into the living room of our apartment, and sat in a rocker. That's when a tsunami of sobriety washed over me.

"We're in charge of a human being."

I don't care how tough you are. You may be a Navy SEAL who specializes in high-altitude skydiving behind enemy lines. You might spend each day making million-dollar split-second stock market decisions. Doesn't matter. Every parent melts the moment he or she feels the full force of parenthood.

I did.

How did I get myself into this? I retraced my steps. First came love, then came marriage, then the *discussions* of a baby carriage. Somehow during the nine-month expansion project, the reality of fatherhood didn't dawn on me. Women are nodding and smiling. "Never underestimate the density of a man," you say. True. But moms have an advantage: thirty-six weeks of reminders elbowing around inside them. Our kick in the gut comes later. But it does come. And for me it came in the midnight quiet of an apartment living room in downtown Rio de Janeiro, Brazil, as I held a human being in my arms.

The semitruck of parenting comes loaded with fears. We fear failing the child, forgetting the child. Will we have enough money? Enough answers? Enough diapers? It's enough to keep a parent awake at night.

And even though we learn to cope, an apiary of dangers buzzes in the background. Consider the mom who called me one evening. A custody battle rages around her ten-year-old son. The courts, the father, the mother, the lawyers—they're stretching the boy like taffy. She wonders if her child will survive the ordeal.

At least she knows where her child is. The mother who called our church for prayers doesn't. Her daughter, a high school senior, ran away with a boyfriend. He's into drugs. She's into him. Both are into trouble. The mother begs for help.

Fear distilleries concoct a high-octane brew for parents—a primal, gut-wrenching, pulse-stilling dose. Whether Mom and Dad keep vigil outside a neonatal unit, make weekly visits to a juvenile prison, or hear the crunch of a bike and the cry of a child in the driveway, their reaction is the same: "I have to do something." No parent can sit still while their child suffers.

Jairus couldn't.

> On the other side of the lake the crowds welcomed Jesus, because they had been waiting for him. Then a man named Jairus, a leader of the local synagogue, came and fell at Jesus' feet, pleading with him to come home with him. His only daughter, who was about twelve years old,

> was dying. As Jesus went with him, he was surrounded by the crowds. (Luke 8:40–42 NLT)

Jairus was a Capernaum community leader, "one of the rulers of the synagogue" (Mark 5:22). Mayor, bishop, and ombudsman, all in one. The kind of man a city would send to welcome a celebrity. But when Jairus approached Jesus on the Galilean shoreline, he wasn't representing his village; he was pleading on behalf of his child.

Urgency stripped the formalities from his greeting. He issued no salutation or compliment, just a prayer of panic. Another gospel reads: "[Jairus] fell at his feet, pleading fervently with him. 'My little daughter is dying,' he said. 'Please come and lay your hands on her; heal her so she can live'" (Mark 5:22–23 NLT).

Jairus isn't the only parent to run onto gospel pages on behalf of a child. A mother stormed out of the Canaanite hills, crying, "Mercy, Master, Son of David! My daughter is cruelly afflicted by an evil spirit" (Matt. 15:22 MSG). A father of a seizure-tormented boy sought help from the disciples, then Jesus. He cried out with tears, "Lord, I believe; help my unbelief!" (Mark 9:24).

The Canaanite mother. The father of the epileptic boy. Jairus. These three parents form an unwitting New Testament society: struggling parents of stricken children. They held the end of their rope in one hand and reached toward Christ with the other. In each case Jesus responded. He never turned one away.

His consistent kindness issues a welcome announcement: Jesus heeds the concern in the parent's heart.

After all, our kids were his kids first. "Don't you see that children are GOD's best gift? the fruit of the womb his generous legacy?" (Ps. 127:3 MSG). Before they were ours, they were his. Even as they are ours, they are still his.

We tend to forget this fact, regarding our children as "our" children, as though we have the final say in their health and welfare. We don't. All people are God's people, including the small people who sit at our tables. Wise are the parents who regularly give their children back to God.

Abraham famously modeled this. The father of the faith was also the father of Isaac. Abraham and Sarah waited nearly a century for this child to be born. Of all the gifts God gave them, Isaac was the greatest. Of all the commands God gave Abraham, this one was the hardest: "He said, 'Take your dear son Isaac whom you love and go to the land of Moriah. Sacrifice him there as a burnt offering on one of the mountains that I'll point out to you'" (Gen. 22:2 MSG).

Abraham saddled the donkey, took Isaac and two servants, and traveled to the place of sacrifice. When he saw the mountain in the distance, he instructed the servants to stay and wait. And he made a statement that is worthy of special note: "Stay here with the donkey. My son and I will go over there and worship, and then we will come back to you" (v. 5 NCV).

Look at Abraham's confident "*we* will come back." "Abraham reasoned that if Isaac died, God was able to bring him back to life again. And in a sense, Abraham did receive his son back from the dead" (Heb. 11:19 NLT). God interrupted the sacrifice and spared Isaac.

Jairus was hoping for the same with his daughter. He begged Jesus to come to his home (Luke 8:41). The father wasn't content with long-distance assistance; he wanted Christ beneath his roof, walking through his rooms, standing at the bedside of his daughter. My wife displays this same longing. I will someday ask God, "Why were you so good to my daughters and me?" and he will answer by pointing to Denalyn. "She just kept talking about you and your kids." Denalyn takes regular prayer walks through our house, stepping into each bedroom and living area. She pauses to pray for her daughters and husband. She takes full advantage of the invitation of Lamentations 2:19: "Pour out your heart like water before the face of the Lord. Lift your hands toward Him for the life of your young children."

Parents, we can do this. We can be loyal advocates, stubborn intercessors. We can take our parenting fears to Christ. In fact, if we don't, we'll take our fears out on our kids. Fear turns some parents into paranoid prison guards who monitor every minute, check the background of every friend. They stifle growth and communicate distrust. A family with no breathing room suffocates a child.

On the other hand, fear can also create permissive parents. For fear that their child will feel too confined or fenced in, they lower all boundaries. High on hugs and low on discipline. They don't realize that appropriate discipline is an expression of love. Permissive parents. Paranoid parents. How can we avoid the extremes? We pray.

Prayer is the saucer into which parental fears are poured to cool. Jesus says so little about parenting, makes no comments about spanking, breastfeeding, sibling rivalry, or schooling. Yet his actions speak volumes about prayer. Each time a parent prays, Christ responds. His big message to moms and dads? Bring your children to me. Raise them in a greenhouse of prayer.

When you send them off for the day, do so with a blessing. When you tell them good night, cover them in prayer. Is your daughter stumped by geography homework? Pray with her about it. Is your son intimidated by the new girl? Pray with him about her. Pray that your children have a profound sense of place in this world and a heavenly place in the next.

Parents, we can't protect children from every threat in life, but we can take them to the Source of life. We can entrust our kids to Christ. Even then, however, our shoreline appeals may be followed by a difficult choice.

As Jairus and Jesus were going to Jairus's home, "a messenger arrived from the home of Jairus, the leader of the synagogue.

He told him, 'Your daughter is dead. There's no use troubling the Teacher now.' But when Jesus heard what had happened, he said to Jairus, 'Don't be afraid. Just have faith, and she will be healed'" (Luke 8:49–50 NLT).

Jairus was whipsawed between the contrasting messages. The first, from the servants: "Your daughter is dead." The second, from Jesus: "Don't be afraid." Horror called from one side. Hope compelled from the other. Tragedy, then trust. Jairus heard two voices and had to choose which one he would heed.

Don't we all?

The hard reality of parenting reads something like this: You can do your best and still stand where Jairus stood. You can protect, pray, and keep all the bogeymen at bay and still find yourself in an ER at midnight or a drug rehab clinic on visitors' Sunday, choosing between two voices: despair and belief. Jairus could have chosen despair. Who would have faulted him for deciding "Enough is enough"? He had no guarantee that Jesus could help. His daughter was dead. Jairus could have walked away. As parents, we're so glad he didn't. We need to know what Jesus will do when we entrust our kids to him.

He *united the household*. "When Jesus went to the house, he let only Peter, John, James, and the girl's father and mother go inside with him" (Luke 8:51 NCV).

Jesus included the mother. Until this point she had been, for whatever reason, out of the picture. Perhaps she was at her daughter's bedside. Or she might have been at odds with her husband. Crisis can divide a family. The stress of caring for a sick or troubled child can drive a wedge between Mom and Dad. But here, Christ united them. Picture Jesus pausing at the house entrance, gesturing for the distraught mother to join them. He didn't have to do so. He could have hurried in without her. But he wanted Mom and Dad to stand together in the struggle. Jesus gathered the entire, albeit small, household in the presence of the daughter.

And he *banished unbelief.* "Now all wept and mourned for her; but He said, 'Do not weep; she is not dead, but sleeping.' And they ridiculed Him, knowing that she was dead. But He put them all outside" (vv. 52–54).

He commanded doubt to depart and permitted only faith and hope to stay. And in this intimate circle of trust, Jesus "took her by the hand and called, saying, 'Little girl, arise.' Then her spirit returned, and she arose immediately. And He commanded that she be given something to eat. And her parents were astonished" (vv. 54–56).

God has a heart for hurting parents. Should we be surprised? After all, God himself is a father. What parental emotion has he not felt? Are you separated from your child? So was God. Is someone mistreating your child? They mocked and bullied his. Is someone taking advantage of your children? The Son of God was set up by false testimony and betrayed by a greedy follower. Are you forced to watch while your child suffers? God watched his Son on the cross. Do you find yourself wanting to spare your child from all the hurt in the world? God did. But because of his great love for us, "he did not spare his own Son but gave him for us all" (Rom. 8:32 NCV).

"All things" must include courage and hope.

Some of you find the story of Jairus difficult to hear. You prayed the same prayer he did, yet you found yourself in a cemetery facing every parent's darkest night: the death of your child. No pain compares. What hope does the story of Jairus offer you? Jesus resurrected Jairus's child. Why didn't he save yours?

God understands your question. He buried a child too. He hates death more than you do. That's why he killed it. He "abolished death and brought life and immortality to light" (2 Tim. 1:10). For those who trust God, death is nothing more than a transition to heaven. Your child may not be in your arms, but your child is safely in his.

Others of you have been standing for a long time where Jairus stood. You've long since left the water's edge of offered prayer but haven't yet arrived at the household of answered prayer. You've wept a monsoon of tears for your child, enough to summon the attention of every angel and their neighbor to your cause. At times you've felt that a breakthrough was nearing, that Christ was following you to your house. But you're not so sure anymore. You find yourself alone on the path, wondering if Christ has forgotten you and your child.

He hasn't. He never dismisses a parent's prayer. Keep giving your child to God and, in the right time and the right way, God will give your child back to you.

Late that night more than a quarter century ago, I gave my daughter to God. As I rocked her in our just-bought rocker, I remembered the way Abraham had placed Isaac on the altar, and I decided to do the same. Following the centenarian's example, I made our apartment living room my Moriah and lifted my daughter toward heaven. *I can't raise this girl,* I confessed, *but you can. I give her back to you.*

Must have been a sight to behold, a pajama-clad father lifting his blanket-wrapped baby toward the ceiling. But something tells me that a few parents appreciated the gesture. Among them, Abraham, Jairus, and, of course, God.

5

I'm Sinking Fast

"Don't be afraid," he said.

"Take courage. I am here!"

—Matthew 14:27 NLT

Before the flight I'm a midlife version of Tom Cruise in *Top Gun*: wearing an air force helmet, a flight suit, and a smile the size of a watermelon slice. After the flight, Top Gun is undone. I'm as pale as bleached bone. I list to the side, and my big smile has flattened as straight as the tarmac on which we just landed. Chalk up the change to sixty minutes of acrobatics at ten thousand feet.

I occupied the cockpit seat directly behind Lt. Col. Tom McClain. One month shy of retirement he invited me to join him on an orientation flight. The invitation came complete with

- a preflight physical (in which I was measured for the ejection seat);

- a safety briefing (in which I practiced pulling the handle for the ejection seat);
- a few moments hanging in the harness of a training parachute (simulating how I would return to earth after any activation of the ejection seat).

Message to air force public relations: Any way to scale down the ejection-seat discussion? Turns out we didn't use it. No small accomplishment since we dived, rose, and dived again, sometimes with a vertical velocity of ten thousand feet per minute. Can you picture a roller coaster minus the rails? We flew in tandem with another T-6. At one point the two wingtips were separated by seven feet. I don't like to get that close to another person in the shopping mall.

Here's what one hour of aerial somersaults taught me:

- Fighter pilots are underpaid. I have no clue what their salary is, but it's not enough. Anyone willing to protect his country at 600 mph deserves a bonus.
- G's are well named. Funny, I thought the phrase "pulling g's" had to do with gravitational pull against your body. It actually describes the involuntary sound a minister emits during a 360-degree rollover: "G-G-G-Geee!"
- The call sign of the pilot is stenciled on the back of his helmet.

They have such great call signs: Iceman. Buff. Hatchet. Mine was Max. Pretty cool, huh? Col. McClain responds to T-Mac. It appears on the back of his helmet just above the collar line. I know this well. For fifty of the sixty minutes, I stared at his name. I read it forward, then backward, counted the letters, and created an acrostic: T-M-A-C. **T**ell **M**e **A**bout **C**hrist. I couldn't stomach looking anywhere else. The horizon kept bouncing. So did the instrument panel. Closing my eyes only increased the nausea. So I stared at T-Mac. After all, he was the one with nearly six thousand hours of flight time!

Six thousand hours! He's spent more time flying planes than I've spent eating pizza, a thought that occurred to me as I began regretting my dinner from the night before. Six thousand hours! The equivalent of eight months' worth of twenty-four-hour days in the air, time enough to circumnavigate the globe 143 times. No wonder he was smiling when we boarded. This sortie was a bike ride on training wheels. I actually heard him humming during a near-vertical bank turn.

Didn't take me long to figure out where to stare. No more looking down or out. My eyes were on the pilot. If T-Mac was okay, I was okay. I know where to stare in turbulence.

Peter learned the same lesson the hard way. Exchange the plane for a thirty-foot fishing boat, the San Antonio sky for a Galilean sea, and our stories begin to parallel. "But the boat was now in the middle of the sea, tossed by the waves, for the wind was contrary" (Matt. 14:24).

As famous lakes go, Galilee—only thirteen miles at its longest, seven and a half at its widest—is a small, moody one. The diminutive size makes it more vulnerable to the winds that howl out of the Golan Heights. They turn the lake into a blender, shifting suddenly, blowing first from one direction, then another. Winter months bring such storms every two weeks or so, churning the waters for two to three days at a time.[1]

Peter and his fellow storm riders knew they were in trouble. What should have been a sixty-minute cruise became a nightlong battle. The boat lurched and lunged like a kite in a March wind. Sunlight was a distant memory. Rain fell from the night sky in buckets. Lightning sliced the blackness with a silver sword. Winds whipped the sails, leaving the disciples "in the middle of the sea, tossed by the waves." Apt description, perhaps, for your stage in life? Perhaps all we need to do is substitute a couple of nouns . . .

In the middle of a divorce, tossed about by disappointment.

In the middle of debt, tossed about by creditors.

The disciples fought the storm for nine cold, skin-drenching hours. And about 4:00 A.M. the unspeakable happened. They spotted someone coming on the water. " 'A ghost!' they said, crying out in terror" (v. 26 MSG).

They didn't expect Jesus to come to them this way.

Neither do we. We expect him to come in the form of peaceful hymns or Easter Sundays or quiet retreats. We expect to find Jesus in morning devotionals, church suppers, and meditation. We never expect to see him in a bear market, pink slip, lawsuit, foreclosure, or war. We never expect to see him in a storm. But it is in storms that he does his finest work, for it is in storms that he has our keenest attention.

Jesus replied to the disciples' fear with an invitation worthy of inscription on every church cornerstone and residential archway. "'Don't be afraid,' he said. 'Take courage. I am here!'" (v. 27 NLT).

Power inhabits those words. To awaken in an ICU and hear your husband say, "I am here." To lose your retirement yet feel the support of your family in the words "We are here." When a Little Leaguer spots Mom or Dad in the bleachers watching the game, "I am here" changes everything. Perhaps that's why God repeats the "I am here" pledge so often.

> The Lord is near. (Phil. 4:5 NIV)

> I am with you always, to the very end of the age. (Matt. 28:20 NIV)

> Nothing can ever separate us from God's love. Neither death nor life, neither angels nor demons, neither our fears for today nor our worries about tomorrow—not even

> the powers of hell can separate us from God's love. (Rom. 8:38 NLT)

We cannot go where God is not. Look over your shoulder; that's God following you. Look into the storm; that's Christ coming toward you.

Much to Peter's credit, he took Jesus at his word. " 'Lord, if it is You, command me to come to You on the water.' So He said, 'Come.' And when Peter had come down out of the boat, he walked on the water to go to Jesus" (Matt. 14:28–29).

Peter never would have made this request on a calm sea. Had Christ strolled across a lake that was as smooth as mica, Peter would have applauded, but I doubt he would have stepped out of the boat. Storms prompt us to take unprecedented journeys. For a few historic steps and heart-stilling moments, Peter did the impossible. He defied every law of gravity and nature; "he walked on the water to go to Jesus."

A wall of water eclipsed his view. A wind gust snapped the mast with a crack and a slap. A flash of lightning illuminated the lake and the watery Appalachians it had become. Peter shifted his attention away from Jesus and toward the squall, and when he did, he sank like a brick in a pond. Give the storm waters more attention than the Storm Walker and get ready to do the same.

Whether or not storms come, we cannot choose. But where we stare during a storm, that we can choose.

God's call to courage is not a call to naïveté or ignorance. We aren't to be oblivious to the overwhelming challenges that life brings. We're to counterbalance them with long looks at God's accomplishments. "We must pay much closer attention to what we have heard, so that we do not drift away from it" (Heb. 2:1 NASB). Do whatever it takes to keep your gaze on Jesus.

When a friend of mine spent several days in the hospital at the bedside of her husband, she relied on hymns to keep her spirits up. Every few minutes she stepped into the restroom and sang a few verses of "Great Is Thy Faithfulness." Do likewise! Memorize Scripture. Read biographies of great lives. Ponder the testimonies of faithful Christians. Make the deliberate decision to set your hope on him. Courage is always a possibility. You can be brave.

Feed your fears, and your faith will starve.

Feed your faith, and your fears will.

Jeremiah did this. Talk about a person caught in a storm! Slide down the timeline to the left about six hundred years and learn a lesson from this Old Testament prophet. "I am the man who has seen affliction under the rod of [God's] wrath; he has driven and brought me into darkness without any light; surely against me he turns his hand again and again the whole day long" (Lam. 3:1–3 RSV).

Jeremiah was depressed, as gloomy as a giraffe with a neck ache. Jerusalem was under siege, his nation under duress. His world collapsed like a sandcastle in a typhoon. He faulted God for his horrible emotional distress. He also blamed God for his physical ailments. "He [God] has made my flesh and my skin waste away, and broken my bones" (v. 4 RSV).

His body ached. His heart was sick. His faith was puny. "[God] has besieged and enveloped me with bitterness and tribulation" (v. 5 RSV). Jeremiah felt trapped like a man on a dead-end street. "He has walled me about so that I cannot escape; he has put heavy chains on me; though I call and cry for help, he shuts out my prayer; he has blocked my ways with hewn stones, he has made my paths crooked" (vv. 7–9 RSV).

Jeremiah could tell you the height of the waves and the speed of the wind. But then he realized how fast he was sinking. So he shifted his gaze. "But this I call to mind, and therefore I have hope: The steadfast love of the LORD never ceases, his mercies never come to an end; they are new every morning; great is thy faithfulness. 'The LORD is my portion,' says my soul, 'therefore I will hope in him'" (vv. 21–24 RSV).

"But this I call to mind . . ." Depressed, Jeremiah altered his thoughts, shifted his attention. He turned his eyes away from the waves and looked into the wonder of God. He quickly recited a quintet of promises. (I can envision him tapping these out on the five fingers of his hand.)

1. The steadfast love of the Lord never ceases.
2. His mercies never come to an end.
3. They are new every morning.

4. Great is thy faithfulness.
5. The Lord is my portion.

The storm didn't cease, but his discouragement did. So did Peter's. After a few moments of flailing in the water, he turned back to Christ and cried, "'Lord, save me!' Immediately Jesus reached out his hand and caught him. 'You of little faith,' he said, 'why did you doubt?' And when they climbed into the boat, the wind died down" (Matt. 14:30–32 NIV).

Jesus could have stilled this storm hours earlier. But he didn't. He wanted to teach the followers a lesson. Jesus could have calmed your storm long ago too. But he hasn't. Does he also want to teach you a lesson? Could that lesson read something like this: "Storms are not an option, but fear is"?

God has hung his diplomas in the universe. Rainbows, sunsets, horizons, and star-sequined skies. He has recorded his accomplishments in Scripture. We're not talking six thousand hours of flight time. His résumé includes Red Sea openings. Lions' mouths closings. Goliath topplings. Lazarus raisings. Storm stillings and strollings.

His lesson is clear. He's the commander of every storm. Are you scared in yours? Then stare at him. This may be your first flight. But it's certainly not his.

Your pilot has a call sign too: I Am Here.

6

There's a Dragon in My Closet

[Jesus] sank into a pit of suffocating darkness.

—Mark 14:33 MSG

Next time an octopus traps you on the ocean floor, don't despair. Just launch into a flurry of somersaults. Unless you're wrapped in the grip of a fearfully strong arm or two, you'll escape with only a few sucker lesions.

As you ascend to the surface, you might encounter a shark. Don't panic—punch! Pound away at the eyes and gills. They are the most sensitive parts of its body.

Though gorillas can't read your mind, they can lock you in their grasp. The grip of a silverback is padlock tight. Your only hope of escape is to stroke its arm while loudly smacking your lips. Primates are fastidious groomers. Hopefully, the gorilla will interpret your actions as a spa treatment.

If not, things could be worse. You could be falling from the sky in a malfunctioning parachute, trapped in a plummeting elevator, or buried alive in a steel coffin. You could be facing your worst-case scenario. We all have them: situations of ultimate desperation. That's why *The Complete Worst-Case Scenario Survival Handbook*[1] has been such a success.

Thanks to the book, I now know how to react to a grabbing gorilla. The odds of such an occasion are so remote, however, I've lost no sleep over them. I have stayed awake pondering other gloomy possibilities.

Growing senile is one. The thought of growing old doesn't trouble me. Don't mind losing my youth, hair, or teeth. But the thought of losing my mind? Dreadful.

Failing to provide for my family has haunted me. In another worst-case scenario my wife, Denalyn, outlives me and our savings and is destitute, dependent upon the generosity of some kind stranger. She tells me to dismiss such thoughts, that my concerns are folly. Easier said than done, I reply.

These lurking fears. These uninvited Loch Ness monsters. Not pedestrian anxieties of daily deadlines and common colds, but the lingering horror of some inescapable talon. Illogical and inexplicable, perhaps, but also undeniable.

What's your worst fear? A fear of public failure, unemployment, or heights? The fear that you'll never find the right spouse or enjoy good health? The fear of being trapped, abandoned, or forgotten?

These are real fears, born out of legitimate concerns. Yet left unchecked, they metastasize into obsessions. The step between prudence and paranoia is short and steep. Prudence wears a seat belt. Paranoia avoids cars. Prudence washes with soap. Paranoia avoids human contact. Prudence saves for old age. Paranoia hoards even trash. Prudence prepares and plans. Paranoia panics. Prudence calculates the risk and takes the plunge. Paranoia never enters the water.

The words *plunge* and *water* come to mind as I'm writing this chapter while sitting on the edge of a hotel swimming pool. A father and his two small daughters are at play. He's in the water; they jump into his arms. Let me restate that: one jumps; the other ponders. The dry one gleefully watches her sister leap. She dances up and down as the other splashes. But when her dad invites her to do the same, she shakes her head and backs away.

A living parable! How many people spend life on the edge of the pool? Consulting caution. Ignoring faith. Never taking the plunge. Happy to experience life vicariously through others. For fear of the worst, they never enjoy life at its best.

By contrast, their sister jumps. Not with foolish abandon but with belief in the goodness of a father's heart and trust in a father's arms. Such was the choice of Jesus. He did more than speak about fear. He faced it.

The decisive acts of the gospel drama are played out on two stages: Gethsemane's garden and Golgotha's cross. Friday's cross witnessed the severest suffering. Thursday's garden staged the profoundest fear. It was here, amid the olive trees, that Jesus "fell to the ground. He prayed that, if it were possible, the awful hour awaiting him might pass him by. 'Abba, Father,' he cried out, 'everything is possible for you. Please take this cup of suffering away from me. Yet I want your will to be done, not mine'" (Mark 14:35–36 NLT).

Gospel writer Mark paints the picture of Jesus as pale faced and trembling. "Horror . . . came over him" (14:33 NEB). The word *horror* is "used of a man who is rendered helpless, disoriented, who is agitated and anguished by the threat of some approaching event."[2]

Matthew agreed. He described Jesus as

> depressed and confused (Matt. 26:37[3]),
> sorrowful and troubled (RSV),
> anguish[ed] and dismay[ed] (NEB).

We've never seen Christ like this. Not in the Galilean storm, at the demoniac's necropolis, or on the edge of the Nazarene cliff. And never, ever have we read a sentence like this: "He sank into a pit of suffocating darkness" (Mark 14:33 MSG). This is a weighty moment. God has become flesh, and flesh is feeling fear full bore. Why? Of what was Jesus afraid?

It had something to do with a cup. "Please take this cup of suffering away from me." *Cup*, in biblical terminology, was more than a drinking utensil. *Cup* equaled God's anger, judgment, and punishment. When God took pity on apostate Jerusalem, he said, "See, I have taken out of your hand the cup that made you stagger . . . the goblet of my wrath" (Isa. 51:22 NIV). Through Jeremiah, God declared that all nations would drink of the cup of his disgust: "Take from my hand this cup filled to the brim with my anger, and make all the nations to whom I send you drink from it" (Jer. 25:15 NLT). According to John, those who dismiss God "must drink the wine of God's anger. It has been poured full strength into God's cup of wrath. And they will be tormented with fire and burning sulfur in the presence of the holy angels and the Lamb" (Rev. 14:10 NLT).

The cup equaled Jesus' worst-case scenario: to be the recipient of God's wrath. He had never felt God's fury, didn't deserve to. He'd never experienced isolation from his Father; the two had been one for eternity. He'd never known physical death; he was an immortal being. Yet within a few short hours, Jesus would face them all. God would unleash his sin-hating wrath on the sin-covered Son. And Jesus was afraid. Deathly afraid. And what he did with his fear shows us what to do with ours.

He prayed. He told his followers, "Sit here while I go and pray over there" (Matt. 26:36). One prayer was inadequate. "Again, a second time, He went away and prayed . . . and prayed the third time, saying the same words" (vv. 42, 44). He even requested the prayer support of his friends. "Stay awake and pray for strength," he urged (v. 41 NCV).

Jesus faced his ultimate fear with honest prayer.

Let's not overcomplicate this topic. Don't we do so? We prescribe words for prayer, places for prayer, clothing for prayer, postures for prayer; durations, intonations, and incantations. Yet Jesus' garden appeal had none of these. It was brief (twenty-six English words), straightforward ("Please take this cup of suffering away"), and trusting ("Yet I want your will to be done, not mine"). Low on slick and high on authentic. Less a silver-tongued saint in the sanctuary, more a frightened child in a father's lap.

That's it. Jesus' garden prayer is a child's prayer. *Abba*, he prayed, using the homespun word a child would use while scampering up on the lap of Papa.

Prayer is the practice of sitting calmly in God's lap and placing our hands on his steering wheel. He handles the speed and hard curves and ensures safe arrival. And we offer our requests; we ask God to "take this cup away." This cup of disease, betrayal, financial collapse, joblessness, conflict, or senility. Prayer is this simple. And such simple prayer equipped Christ to stare down his deepest fear.

Do likewise. Fight your dragons in Gethsemane's garden. Those persistent, ugly villains of the heart—talk to God about them.

I don't want to lose my spouse, Lord. Help me to fear less and trust you more.

I have to fly tomorrow, Lord, and I can't sleep for fear some terrorist will get on board and take down the plane. Won't you remove this fear?

The bank just called and is about to foreclose on our home. What's going to happen to my family? Can you teach me to trust?

I'm scared, Lord. The doctor just called, and the news is not good. You know what's ahead for me. I give my fear to you.

Be specific about your fears. Identify what "this cup" is and talk to God about it.

Let's pull back the curtains to expose our fears, each and every one. Like vampires, fears can't stand the sunlight. Financial fears, relationship fears, professional fears, safety fears—call them out in prayer. Drag them out by the hand of your mind and make them stand before God and take their comeuppance!

Jesus made his fears public. He "offered up prayers and petitions with fervent cries and tears to the one who could save him from death" (Heb. 5:7 NIV). He prayed loudly enough to be heard and recorded, and he begged his community of friends to pray with him.

His prayer in the garden becomes, for Christians, a picture of the church in action—a place where fears can be verbalized, pronounced, stripped down, and denounced; an escape from the wordless darkness of suppressed frights. A healthy church is where our fears go to die. We pierce them through with Scripture, psalms of celebration and lament. We melt them in the sunlight of confession. We extinguish them with the waterfall of worship, choosing to gaze at God, not our dreads.

The next time you find yourself facing a worst-case moment, do this. Verbalize your angst to a trusted circle of God-seekers. This is an essential step. Find your version of Peter, James, and John. (One hopes yours will stay awake longer.) The big deal (and good news) is this: You needn't live alone with your fear.

Besides, what if these fears of yours are nothing more than the devil's hoax? A hell-hatched, joy-stealing prank?

I have a friend who was dreading a letter from the IRS. According to their early calculation, he owed them money, money he did not have. He was told to expect a letter detailing the amount. When the letter arrived, his courage failed him. He couldn't bear to open it, so the envelope sat on his desk for five days while he writhed in dread. How much could it be? Where would he get the funds? For how long would he be sent to prison? Finally he summoned the gumption to open the envelope. He found, not a bill to be paid, but a check to be cashed. The IRS, as it turned out, owed him money! He had wasted five days on needless fear. There are very few monsters who warrant the fear we have of them.

As followers of God, you and I have a huge asset. We know everything is going to turn out all right. Christ hasn't budged from his throne, and Romans 8:28 hasn't evaporated from the Bible. Our problems have always been his possibilities. The kidnapping of Joseph resulted in the preservation of his family. The persecution of Daniel led to a cabinet position. Christ entered the world by a surprise pregnancy and redeemed it through his unjust murder. Dare we believe what the Bible teaches? That no disaster is ultimately fatal?

The apostle Paul penned his final words in the bowels of a Roman prison, chained to a guard—within earshot of his executioner's footsteps. Worst-case scenario? Not from Paul's perspective. "God's looking after me, keeping me safe in the kingdom of heaven. All praise to him, praise forever!" (2 Tim. 4:18 MSG).

Paul chose to trust his Father.

By the way, I'm happy to report that the poolside girl has chosen to believe hers. After extensive coaxing from her dad and coaching from her sister, she held her nose and jumped. Last tally, she's taken at least a dozen plunges. Good for her. Another fear has fallen victim to trust.

7

This Brutal Planet

Do not fear those who kill the body
but cannot kill the soul.
—Matthew 10:28

One of the greatest golfers in the history of the sport sat down to eat his breakfast never suspecting it would be his last. Byron Nelson had slept well the night before, better than he had in days. He had showered, shaved, and then smiled when his wife, Peggy, announced the meal of the morning: sausage, biscuits, and eggs.

He was ninety-four years old, sixty-one years removed from the streak: eleven consecutive PGA tournament victories. No other pro golfer comes close to matching that (Tiger Woods is in second place with a streak of seven). Nelson's record stands out like an oak tree in a wheat field. He retired a year later and bought a ranch near Fort Worth, Texas, where he lived peacefully until God called him home September 26, 2006.

After washing the dishes, he sat down to listen to a favorite Christian radio broadcast. Peggy left for Bible study at the church. ("I'm so proud of you," he told her.) She returned a few hours later to find him on the floor. No sign of pain or struggle. His good heart had just stopped.[1]

Russia of the early 1950s needed little excuse to imprison her citizens.

Let a person question a decision of Stalin or speak against the Communist regime, and he could find himself walking the frozen tundra behind the barbed wires of a Soviet concentration camp. Boris Kornfeld did. No known record of his crime survives, only the sketchy details of his life. Born a Jew. Trained as a physician and befriended by a believer in Christ.

With ample time on their hands, the two men engaged in long, rigorous discussions. Kornfeld began to connect the promised Messiah of the old covenant with the Nazarene of the new. Following Jesus went against every fiber of his ancestry, but in the end he chose to do so.

The decision cost him his life.

He saw a guard stealing bread from a dying man. Prior to his conversion, Kornfeld never would have reported the crime. Now his conscience compelled him to do so. It was only a matter of time before the other guards would get even. Kornfeld, even in danger, was at complete peace. For the first time in his life, he had no fear of death or eternity. His only desire was to tell someone about his discovery before he lost his life.

An opportunity came in the form of a cancer patient, a fellow prisoner who was recovering from abdominal surgery. Left alone with him in the recovery room, Kornfeld urgently whispered his story. He poured out every detail. The young man was stirred, yet so groggy from the anesthesia that he fell asleep. When he awoke, he asked to see the physician. It was too late. During the night someone had dealt the doctor eight blows on the head with a plasterer's hammer. Colleagues had tried to save his life but couldn't.[2]

Byron Nelson and Boris Kornfeld embraced the same convictions. They anchored their hopes to the same rock and set their sights on the same heaven and trusted the same Savior. Yet one passed into heaven on a pathway of peace, the other through a maelstrom of brutality.

Given the choice, I'd go out like Mr. Nelson.

The unnamed heroes of Hebrews would have as well. Their stories occupy a curious paragraph toward the end of the patriarch parade. They follow the better-known names of Abel, who though "being dead still speaks" (Heb. 11:4); Enoch, who "did not see death" (v. 5); Noah, who "became heir of the righteousness" (v. 7); Abraham and Sarah, whose descendants are as "innumerable as the sand which is by the seashore" (v. 12).

A person might read this far and draw a conclusion. God rewards faithful lives with serenity and storied legacies. Live well. Live and die peacefully. Right? Then verses 35–37 present the hard side: "Others were tortured, not accepting deliverance, that they might obtain a better resurrection. Still others had trials of mockings and scourgings, yes, and of chains and imprisonment. They were stoned, they were sawn in two, were tempted, were slain with the sword. They wandered about in sheepskins and goatskins, being destitute, afflicted, tormented."

Contrary to what we'd hope, good people aren't exempt from violence. The bloodthirsty and wicked don't skip over the heavenbound. We aren't insulated. But neither are we intimidated. Jesus has a word or two about this brutal world: "Do not fear those who kill the body but cannot kill the soul" (Matt. 10:28).

The disciples needed this affirmation. Jesus had just told them to expect scourging, trials, death, hatred, and persecution (vv. 17–23). Not the kind of locker-room pep talk that rallies the team. To their credit none defected. Perhaps they didn't because of the fresh memory of Jesus' flexed muscles in the graveyard. Jesus had taken his disciples to "the other side into the country of the Gadarenes, [where] two men who were demon-possessed met Him as they were coming out of the tombs. They were so extremely violent that no one could pass by that way. And they cried out, saying, 'What business do we have with each other,

Son of God? Have You come here to torment us before the time?'" (Matt. 8:28–29 NASB).

The most dramatic and immediate reactions to the presence of God on earth emerged from demons like these—the numberless, invisible, sexless, fiendish djinns of Satan. These two men were demon-possessed and, consequently, "extremely violent." People walked wide detours around the cemetery to avoid them.

Not Jesus. He marched in as if he owned the place. The stunned demons never expected to see Jesus here in the devil's digs on the foreign side of Galilee, the region of pagans and pigs. Jews avoided such haunts. Jesus didn't.

The demons and Jesus needed no introduction. They had battled it out somewhere else, and the demons had no interest in a rematch. They didn't even put up a fight. "Have you come to punish us before our time?" (v. 29 CEV). Backpedaling. Stuttering. Translation? "We know you will put it to us in the end, but do we get double trouble in the meantime?" They crumpled like stringless puppets. Pathetic, their appeal: "Please send us into those pigs!" (v. 31 CEV).

Jesus did so. "Move," he exorcised. No shout, scream, incantation, dance, incense, or demand. Just one small word. He who sustains the worlds with a word directs demonic traffic with the same.

The contest between good and evil lasted a matter of seconds. Christ is fire, and demons are rats on the ship. They scurried overboard at first heat.

This is the balance on which Jesus writes the check of courage: "Do not fear those who kill the body but cannot kill the soul." You indwell the garrison of God's guardianship. "Can anything separate us from the love Christ has for us? Can troubles or problems or sufferings or hunger or nakedness or danger or violent death? . . . Nothing above us, nothing below us, nor anything else in the whole world will ever be able to separate us from the love of God that is in Christ Jesus our Lord" (Rom. 8:35, 39 NCV).

Evildoers have less chance of hurting you if you aren't already a victim. "Fearing people is a dangerous trap, but trusting the LORD means safety" (Prov. 29:25 NLT). Remember, "his angels . . . guard you" (Ps. 91:11 NIV). He is your "refuge" (Ps. 62:8), your "hiding place" (Ps. 32:7), your "fortress" (2 Sam. 22:2–3). "The LORD is on my side; I will not fear. What can man do to me?" (Ps. 118:6). Satan cannot reach you without passing through him.

Then what are we to make of the occasions Satan does reach us? How are we supposed to understand the violence listed in Hebrews 11 or the tragic end of Boris Kornfeld? Or, most supremely, how are we to understand the suffering of Jesus? Ropes. Whips. Thorns. Nails. These trademarked his final moments. Do you hear the whip slapping against his back, ripping sinew from bone? Thirty-nine times the leather slices, first the air, then the skin. Jesus clutches the post and groans, battered by wave after wave of violence. Soldiers force a thorny wreath over his brow, sting his face with slaps, coat it with saliva. They load a beam onto his shoulders and force him to march up a hill. Jesus shouldered his own tool of execution. The cross.

A calmer death would have sufficed. A single drop of blood could have redeemed humankind. Shed his blood, silence his breath, still his pulse, but be quick about it. Plunge a sword into his heart. Take a dagger to his neck. Did the atonement for sin demand six hours of violence?

No, but his triumph over sadism did. Jesus once and for all displayed his authority over savagery. Evil may have her moments, but they will be brief. Satan unleashed his meanest demons on God's Son. He tortured every nerve ending and inflicted every misery. Yet the master of death could not destroy the Lord of life. Heaven's best took hell's worst and turned it into hope.

I pray God spares you such evil. May he grant you the long life and peaceful passage of a Byron Nelson. But if he doesn't, if you "have been given not only the privilege of trusting in Christ but also the privilege of suffering for him" (Phil. 1:29 NLT), remember, God wastes no pain.

Consider Boris Kornfeld, the Russian physician bludgeoned to death because of his convictions. Though the doctor died, his testimony survived. The man with whom he spoke never forgot the conversation.

There, in the quiet camp hospital recovery room, the doctor

sat by his patient's bedside dispensing compassion and peace. Dr. Kornfeld passionately related the story of his conversion to Christianity, his words flavored with conviction. The patient was hot and feverish, yet alert enough to ponder Dr. Kornfeld's words. He would later write that he sensed a "mystical knowledge" in the doctor's voice.

The "mystical knowledge" transformed the young patient. He embraced Kornfeld's Christ and later celebrated in verse with this joyous affirmation: "God of Universe! I believe again!"[3]

The patient survived the camps and began to write about his prison experience, disclosing the gulag horror. One exposé after another: *One Day in the Life of Ivan Denisovich*, *The Gulag Archipelago*, *Live Not by Lies*. The collapse of communism in the Soviet Union and Eastern Europe is attributed by some at least partially to his writings. But were it not for the suffering of Kornfeld, we'd never have known the brilliance of his young convert: Aleksandr Solzhenitsyn.

What man meant for evil, God, yet again, used for good.

8

Make-Believe Money

Do not fear, little flock, for it is your Father's good pleasure to give you the kingdom.

—Luke 12:32

A Monopoly champion sits in your office. The Michael Phelps of the game board. The Pelé of the Boardwalk. He spends all day every day slam-dunking the competition, collecting houses, Park Places, and make-believe money the way Solomon collected wives. He never goes to jail, always passes Go, and has permanent addresses on Illinois and Kentucky Avenues. If the Fortune 500 ranked Monopoly billionaires, this guy would out-Buffett Warren Buffett. No one has more money than he.

And he wants you to help him invest it. You are, after all, a financial planner. You speak the language of stocks and annuities, have ample experience with IRAs, mutual funds, and securities. But all your experience didn't prepare you for this request. Yet here he sits in your office, encircled by bags of pink cash and little plastic buildings. Invest Monopoly earnings?

"I have 314 Park Places, 244 Boardwalks, and enough Reading Railroads to circle the globe like thread on a spool."

Is this guy for real? You do your best to be polite. "Seems you've amassed quite a Monopoly fortune."

He crosses his arms and smiles. "Indeed I have. And I'm ready for you to put it to work. It's time for me to sit back and take it easy. Let someone else monopolize Monopoly for a while."

You take another look at his stacks of funny money and toy real estate and abandon all tact. "Sir, you're crazy. Your currency has no value. Your cash has no clout. Outside of your game, it's worthless. I'm sorry to tell you this, but you've made a foolish mistake. In fact, you are a fool."

Strong language. But if you choose to use it, you are in the company of God.

> And [Jesus] told them this parable: "The ground of a certain rich man yielded an abundant harvest. He thought to himself, 'What shall I do? I have no place to store my crops.'
>
> "Then he said, 'This is what I'll do. I will tear down my barns and build bigger ones, and there I will store my surplus grain. And I'll say to myself, "You have plenty of grain laid up for many years. Take life easy; eat, drink and be merry."'

"But God said to him, 'You fool! This very night your life will be demanded from you. Then who will get what you have prepared for yourself?'

"This is how it will be with whoever stores up things for themselves but is not rich toward God." (Luke 12:16–21 NIV)

He seemed to be a decent fellow, this wealthy farmer. Sharp enough to turn a profit, savvy enough to enjoy a windfall. For all we know, he made his fortune honestly. No mention is made of exploitation or embezzlement. He put his God-given talent to making talents and succeeded. Flush with success, he resolved to learn a lesson from the fable of the ant and the grasshopper.

The grasshopper, you'll remember, wondered why the ant worked so hard in the summer day. "Why not come and chat with me instead of toiling in that way?" The ant explained his labor: "I'm helping to lay up food for the winter and recommend you do the same." But the grasshopper preferred to flitter rather than work. So while the ant prepared, the grasshopper played. And when winter brought its harsh winds and barren fields, the ant nibbled on corn while the grasshopper stood on the street corner holding a cardboard sign: "Any work will do. I'll hop right to it."

The tycoon in Jesus' story wasn't about to play the role of the grasshopper. No food lines or soup kitchens for him. And no food lines or soup kitchens for us either. We empathize with the fecund farmer. Truth be told, we want to learn from his success. Has he written a book (*Bigger Barns for Retirement*)? Does he conduct seminars ("Recession-Proof Your Barn in Twelve Easy Steps")? Doesn't the barn-stuffer model responsible planning? And yet Jesus crowns him with the pointy hat of the dunce. Where did the guy mess up? Jesus answers by populating three paragraphs with a swarm of personal pronouns. Note the heart of the investor in this paraphrase of verses 18–19 (emphasis added):

> And *he* thought to *himself*, saying, "What shall *I* do since *I* have no room to store *my* crops?" So *he* said, "*I* will do this: *I* will pull down *my* barns and build greater ones, and there *I* will store all *my* crops and all *my* goods. And *I* will say to *my* soul, 'Soul, *you* have many goods laid up for many years; take *your* ease, eat, drink, and be merry.'"

This rich man indwelled a one-room house of mirrors. He looked north, south, east, and west and saw the same individual—himself. No *they*. No *thee*. Just *me*. Even when he said *you*, he spoke to himself. "You have many goods. Take your ease."

And so he did. He successfully hoarded enough stuff so he could wine, dine, and recline. He moved to Scottsdale, bought a five-bedroom split-level on the third fairway of the country club. He unpacked the moving vans, set up his bank accounts, pulled on his swimming trunks, and dove into the backyard pool. Too bad he forgot to fill it with water. He popped his skull on the concrete and woke up in the presence of God, who was anything but impressed with his portfolio. "Fool! This night your soul will be required of you; then whose will those things be which you have provided?" (Luke 12:20).

The rich fool went to the wrong person ("He thought to himself") and asked the wrong question ("What shall I do?"). His error was not that he planned but rather that his plans didn't include God. Jesus criticized not the man's affluence but his arrogance, not the presence of personal goals but the absence of God in those goals. What if he'd taken his money to the right person (God) with the right question ("What do you want me to do?")?

Accumulation of wealth is a popular defense against fear. Since we fear losing our jobs, health care, or retirement benefits, we amass possessions, thinking the more we have, the safer we are. The same insecurity motivated Babel's tower builders. The nations that spread out after Noah's flood decided to circle their wagons. "Come, let us build ourselves a city, and a tower whose top is in the heavens; let us make a name for ourselves, lest we be scattered abroad over the face of the whole earth" (Gen. 11:4).

Do you detect the fear in those words? The people feared being scattered and separated. Yet rather than turn to God, they turned to stuff. They accumulated and stacked. They collected and built. News of their efforts would reach the heavens and keep their enemies at a distance. The city motto of Babel was this: "The more you hoard, the safer you are." So they hoarded. They heaped stones and mortar and bricks and mutual funds and IRAs and savings accounts. They stockpiled pensions, possessions, and property. Their tower of stuff grew so tall they got neck aches looking at it.

"We are safe!" they announced at the ribbon-cutting ceremony.

"No you aren't," God corrected. And the Babel builders began to babble. The city of one language became the glossolalia of the United Nations minus the interpreters. Doesn't God invoke identical correction today? We engineer stock and investment levies, take cover behind the hedge of hedge funds. We trust annuities and pensions to the point that balance statements determine our mood levels. But then come the Katrina-level recessions and downturns, and the confusion begins all over again.

If there were no God, stuff-trusting would be the only appropriate response to an uncertain future. But there is a God. And this God does not want his children to trust money. He responded to the folly of the rich man with a flurry of "Do not worry" appeals. "Do not worry about your life. . . . Do not seek what you should eat or what you should drink, nor have an anxious mind" (Luke 12:22, 29).

Giving characterizes God's creation. From the first page of Scripture, he is presented as a philanthropic creator. He produces in pluralities: star*s*, plant*s*, bird*s*, and animal*s*. Every gift arrives in bulk, multiples, and medleys. God begets Adam and Eve into a "liturgy of abundance"[1] and tells them to follow suit: "Be fruitful and multiply" (Gen. 1:28).

Scrooge didn't create the world; God did.

Psalm 104 celebrates this lavish creation with twenty-three verses of itemized blessings: the heavens and the earth, the waters and streams and trees and birds and goats and wine and oil and bread and people and lions. God is the source of "innumerable teeming things, living things both small and great. . . . These all wait for You, that You may give them their food in due season" (vv. 25, 27).

And he does. God is the great giver. The great provider. The fount of every blessing. Absolutely generous and utterly dependable. The resounding and recurring message of Scripture is clear: God owns it all. God shares it all. Trust him, not stuff!

> Command those who are rich in this present age not to be haughty, nor to trust in uncertain riches but in the living God, who gives us richly all things to enjoy. Let them do good, that they be rich in good works, ready to give, willing to share, storing up for themselves a good

> foundation for the time to come, that they may lay hold on eternal life. (1 Tim. 6:17–19)

Are you "rich in this present age"? If you have the resources and education to read this book, you are. Almost half the world—more than three billion people—live on less than $2.50 a day.[2] If your income is higher, then you are rich, and your affluence demands double vigilance.

Do not be haughty . . . Do not think for a moment that you had anything to do with your accumulation. Scripture makes one thing clear. Your stocks, cash, and 401(k)? They are not yours.

> To the LORD your God belong the heavens, even the highest heavens, the earth and everything in it. (Deut. 10:14 NIV)

> "The silver is mine and the gold is mine," declares the LORD Almighty. (Hag. 2:8 NIV)

The rich fool in Jesus' story missed this point. The wise woman Jesus spotted in the temple did not. "Then a poor widow came and dropped in two small coins. Jesus called his disciples to him and said, 'I tell you the truth, this poor widow has given more than all the others who are making contributions. For they gave a tiny part of their surplus, but she, poor as she is, has given everything she had to live on'" (Mark 12:42–44 NLT).

The dear woman was down to her last pennies, yet rather

than spend them on bread, she returned them to God. Wall Street financial gurus would have urged her to cut back on her giving. In fact, the investment counselors would have applauded the investment strategy of the barn builder and discouraged the generosity of the lady. Jesus did just the opposite. His hero of financial stewardship was a poor woman who placed her entire portfolio in the offering plate.

God owns everything and gives us all things to enjoy. He is a good shepherd to us, his little flock. Trust him, not stuff. Move from the fear of scarcity to the comfort of provision. Less hoarding, more sharing. "Do good . . . be rich in good works, ready to give, willing to share."

And, most of all, replace fear of the coming winter with faith in the living God. After all, it's just Monopoly money. It all goes back in the box when the game is over.

9

Scared to Death

Don't let your hearts be troubled. Trust in God,
and trust also in me. . . . I will come and get you,
so that you will always be with me where I am.

—John 14:1, 3 NLT

Once, in a dream, I encountered a man who was wearing a fedora and a corduroy coat. He was the classroom version of Indiana Jones: distinguished, professorial, strong jawed, and kind eyed. He frequented funerals. Apparently I did as well, for the dream consisted of one memorial after another—at funeral homes, chapels, gravesides. He never removed his hat. I never asked him why he wore it, but I did ask him to explain his proverbial presence at interments.

"I come to take people to their eternal home." In waking moments this explanation would have prompted a call to the FBI for a background check. But this was a dream, and dreams permit oddities, so I didn't probe. I didn't ask about the source of his list or the mode of his transport. I didn't think it odd to see the fedora at funerals. But I did think it strange to run into the man on a crowded street.

Think Thanksgiving Day parade or Fourth of July festival. A people-packed avenue. "I'm surprised to see you here," I told him. He didn't reply.

I saw one of my friends standing nearby. A good man, a widower, up in years, poor in health. Suddenly I understood the presence of the fedora-clad angel.

"You've come for my friend."

"No."

Then the dream did what only dreams can do. It dismissed everyone but the visitor and me. The crowded sidewalk became a quiet boulevard, so quiet I couldn't mistake his next words.

"Max, I came for you."

Curiously, I didn't resist, object, or run. I did, however, make a request. When he agreed, the street suddenly filled, and I began going from person to person saying goodbye. I told no one about the angel or the hat or where I was going. As far as others knew, they would see me again tomorrow.

But I knew better, and because I did, the world righted itself. As if the lens of life had been out of focus, with a twist the picture cleared. Follies and offenses were forgotten. Love was amplified. I shook the hand of a harsh critic, gave my wallet to a beggar. I embraced a few coldhearted and hot-tempered folks. And to my dear ones, my wife and daughters, I gave a prayer. A simpler prayer I could not have prayed. *Stay strong. Trust Christ.*

And then the dream was done. I was awake. And within an hour I had recorded every memory of the dream.

It's lingered with me for years. Like a favorite song or sweater, I return to it. Can't say I do the same with other dreams. But this one stands out because it resonates with a deep desire, a desire you might share: to face death unafraid. To die without fright or a fight . . . perhaps with a smile.

Impossible? Some have said so.

Aristotle called death the thing to be feared most because "it appears to be the end of everything."[1] Jean-Paul Sartre asserted that death "removes all meaning from life."[2] Robert Green Ingersoll, one of America's most outspoken agnostics, could offer no words of hope at his brother's funeral. He said, "Life is a narrow vale between the cold and barren peaks of two eternities. We strive in vain to look beyond the heights."[3] The pessimism of French philosopher François Rabelais was equally arctic. He made this sentence his final one: "I am going to the great Perhaps."[4]

Such sad, depressing language! If death is nothing more than "the end of everything," "barren peaks," and "the great Perhaps," what is the possibility of dying bravely? But what if the philosophers missed it? Suppose death is different from how they thought of it, less a curse and more a passageway, not a crisis to be avoided but a corner to be turned? What if the cemetery is not the dominion of the Grim Reaper but the domain of the Soul Keeper, who will someday announce, "O dwellers in the dust, awake and sing for joy!" (Isa. 26:19 RSV)?

This is the promise of Christ: "Don't let your hearts be troubled. Trust in God, and trust also in me. There is more than enough room in my Father's home. If this were not so, would I have told you that I am going to prepare a place for you? When everything is ready, I will come and get you, so that you will always be with me where I am" (John 14:1–3 NLT).

While Jesus' words sound comforting to us, they sounded radical to his first-century audience. He was promising to accomplish a feat no one dared envision or imagine. He would return from the dead and rescue his followers from the grave.

Traditional Judaism was divided on the topic of resurrection. "For Sadducees say that there is no resurrection—and no angel or spirit; but the Pharisees confess both" (Acts 23:8). The Sadducees saw the grave as a tragic, one-way trip into Sheol. No escape. No hope. No possibility of parole. "The living know that they will die, but the dead know nothing" (Eccl. 9:5 NIV).

The Pharisees envisioned a resurrection, yet the resurrection was spiritual, not physical. "There are no traditions about prophets being raised to a new bodily life. . . . However exalted Abraham, Isaac, and Jacob may have been in Jewish thought, nobody imagined they had been raised from the dead."[5]

Ancient Greek philosophy used different language but resulted in identical despair. Their map of death included the

River Styx and the boatman Charon. Upon death, the soul of the individual would be ferried across the river and released into a sunless afterlife of bodiless spirits, shades, and shadows.

This was the landscape into which Jesus entered. Yet he walked into this swamp of uncertainty and built a sturdy bridge. He promised not just an afterlife but a better life.

"There are many rooms in my Father's home, and I am going to prepare a place for you." We Westerners might miss the wedding images, but you can bet your sweet chuppah that Jesus' listeners didn't. This was a groom-to-bride promise. Upon receiving the permission of both families, the groom returned to the home of his father and built a home for his bride. He "prepared a place."

By promising to do the same for us, Jesus elevates funerals to the same hope level as weddings. From his perspective the trip to the cemetery and the walk down the aisle warrant identical excitement.

Weddings are great news! So, says Jesus, are burials. Both celebrate a new era, name, and home. In both the groom walks the bride away on his arm. Jesus is your coming groom. "I will come and get you." He will meet you at the altar. Your final glimpse of life will trigger your first glimpse of him.

But how can we be sure he will keep this pledge? Do we have any guarantee that his words are more than empty poetry or vain superstition? Dare we set our hope and hearts in the hands of a small-town Jewish carpenter? The answer rests in the Jerusalem graveyard. If Jesus' tomb is empty, then his promise is not. Leave it to the apostle Paul to reduce the logic to a single sentence: "There is an order to this resurrection: Christ was raised as the first of the harvest; then all who belong to Christ will be raised when he comes back" (1 Cor. 15:23 NLT).

Paul was writing to Corinthian Christians, people who had been schooled in the Greek philosophy of a shadowy afterlife. Someone was convincing them that corpses couldn't be raised, neither theirs nor Christ's. The apostle couldn't bear such a thought. "Let me go over the Message with you one final time" (1 Cor. 15:1 MSG). With the insistence of an attorney in closing arguments, he reviewed the facts: "[Jesus] was raised from death on the third day . . . he presented himself alive to Peter . . . his closest followers . . . more than five hundred of his followers . . . James . . . the rest of those he commissioned . . . and . . . finally . . . to me" (vv. 4–8 MSG).

Line up the witnesses, he offered. Call them out one by one. Let each person who saw the resurrected Christ say so. Better pack a lunch and clear your calendar, for more than five hundred testifiers are willing to speak up.

Do you see Paul's logic? If one person claimed a post-cross encounter with Christ, disregard it. If a dozen people offered depositions, chalk it up to mob hysteria. But fifty people? A hundred? Three hundred? When one testimony expands to hundreds, disbelief becomes belief.

Paul knew, not handfuls, but hundreds of eyewitnesses. Peter. James. John. The followers, the gathering of five hundred disciples, and Paul himself. They saw Jesus. They saw him physically.

They saw him factually. They didn't see a phantom or experience a sentiment. Grave eulogies often include such phrases as "She'll live on forever in my heart." Jesus' followers weren't saying this. They saw Jesus "in the flesh."

When he appeared to the disciples, he assured them, "It is I myself!" (Luke 24:39 NIV). The Emmaus-bound disciples saw nothing extraordinary about his body. His feet touched the ground. His hands touched the bread. They thought he was a fellow pilgrim until "their eyes were opened" (Luke 24:31 NIV). Mary saw Jesus in the garden and called him "sir" (John 20:15 NIV). The disciples saw Jesus cooking fish on the shore. The resurrected Christ did physical deeds in a physical body. "I am not a ghost," he informed (Luke 24:39 NLT). "Handle Me and see, for a spirit does not have flesh and bones as you see I have" (Luke 24:39).

Jesus experienced a physical and factual resurrection. And—here it is—because he did, we will too! "Christ was raised as the first of the harvest; then all who belong to Christ will be raised when he comes back" (1 Cor. 15:23 NLT).

Aristotle was wrong. Death is not to be feared. Sartre was mistaken. Your last moment is not your worst. The Greek itinerary was inaccurate. Charon won't ferry you into oblivion. Five hundred witnesses left a still-resounding testimony: It's safe to die.

So let's die with faith. Let's allow the resurrection to sink into the fibers of our hearts and define the way we look at the grave. Let it "free those who were like slaves all their lives because of their fear of death" (Heb. 2:15 NCV).

Death—no need to dread it or ignore it. Because of Christ, you can face it.

I did. As heart surgeries go, mine was far from the riskiest. But any procedure that requires four hours of probes inside your heart is enough to warrant an added prayer. So on the eve of my surgery, Denalyn and I, with some kind friends, offered our share. We were staying at a hotel adjacent to the Cleveland Clinic in Ohio. We asked God to bless the doctors and watch over the nurses. After we chatted a few minutes, they wished me well and said goodbye. I needed to go to bed early. But before I could sleep, I wanted to offer one more prayer . . . alone.

I took the elevator down to the lobby and found a quiet corner and began to think. *What if the surgery goes awry? What if this is my final night on earth? Is there anyone with whom I should make my peace? Do I need to phone any person and make amends?* I couldn't think of anyone. (So if you are thinking I should have called you, sorry. Perhaps we should talk.)

Next I wrote letters to my wife and daughters, each beginning with the sentence "If you are reading this, something went wrong in the surgery."

Then God and I had the most honest of talks. We began with a good review of my first half century. The details would bore you, but they entertained us. I thanked him for grace beyond measure and for a wife who descended from the angels. My tabulation of blessings could have gone on all night and threatened to do just that. So I stopped and offered this prayer: *I'm in good hands, Lord. The doctors are prepared; the staff is experienced. But even with the best of care, things happen. This could be my final night in this version of life, and I'd like you to know, if that's the case, I'm okay.*

And I went to bed. And slept like a baby. As things turned out, no angel came. I saw no fedora. I recovered from the surgery, and here I am, strong as ever, still pounding away at the computer keyboard. One thing is different, though. This matter of dying bravely?

I think I will.

May you do the same.

10

Caffeinated Life

I am leaving you with a gift—peace of mind and heart. And the peace I give is a gift the world cannot give. So don't be troubled or afraid.

—John 14:27 NLT

If only we could order life the way we order gourmet coffee. Wouldn't you love to mix and match the ingredients of your future?

"Give me a tall, extra-hot cup of adventure, cut the dangers, with two shots of good health."

"I'll go with a grande happy-latte, with a dollop of love, sprinkled with Caribbean retirement."

Take me to *that* coffee shop. Too bad it doesn't exist. Truth is, life often hands us a concoction entirely different from the one we requested. Ever feel as though the barista-from-above called your name and handed you a cup of unwanted stress?

"Joe Jones, enjoy your early retirement. Looks as if it comes with marital problems and inflation."

"Mary Adams, you wanted four years of university education, then kids. You'll be having kids first. Congratulations on your pregnancy."

Life comes caffeinated with surprises. Modifications. Transitions. Alterations. You move down the ladder, out of the house, over for the new guy, up through the system. All this moving. Some changes welcome, others not. And in those rare seasons when you think the world has settled down, watch out. One seventy-seven-year-old recently told a friend of mine, "I've had a good life. I am enjoying my life now, and I am looking forward to the future." Two weeks later a tornado ripped through the region, taking the lives of his son, daughter-in-law, grandson, and daughter-in-law's mother. We just don't know, do we? On our list of fears, the fear of what's next demands a prominent position. We might request a decaffeinated life, but we don't get it. The disciples didn't.

"I am going away" (John 14:28).

Imagine their shock when they heard Jesus say those words on the night of the Passover celebration, Thursday evening, in a certain upper room. Christ and his friends had just enjoyed a calm dinner in the midst of a chaotic week. They had reason for optimism: Jesus' popularity was soaring. In three short years the crowds had lifted Christ to their shoulders . . . he was the hope of the common man.

The disciples were talking kingdom rhetoric, ready to rain down fire on their enemies, jockeying for positions in the cabinet of Christ. They envisioned a restoration of Israel to her days of glory. No more Roman occupation or foreign oppression. This was the parade to freedom, and Jesus was leading it.

And now this? Jesus said, "I am going away." The announcement stunned them.

Christ handed the disciples a cup of major transition, and they tried to hand it back. Wouldn't we do the same? Yet who succeeds? What person passes through life surprise-free? If you don't want change, go to a soda machine; that's the only place you won't find any. Remember the summary of Solomon?

> For everything there is a season,
> a time for every activity under heaven.
> A time to be born and a time to die.
> A time to plant and a time to harvest.
> A time to kill and a time to heal.
> A time to tear down and a time to build up.
> A time to cry and a time to laugh.
> A time to grieve and a time to dance.
> A time to scatter stones and a time to gather stones.
> A time to embrace and a time to turn away.
> A time to search and a time to quit searching.
> A time to keep and a time to throw away.

A time to tear and a time to mend.
A time to be quiet and a time to speak.
A time to love and a time to hate.
A time for war and a time for peace. (Eccl. 3:1–8 NLT)

I count twenty-eight different seasons. Birth, death, lamenting, cheering, loving, hating, embracing, separating, and more. God dispenses life the way he manages his cosmos: through seasons. When it comes to the earth, we understand God's management strategy. Nature needs winter to rest and spring to awaken. We don't dash into underground shelters at the sight of spring's tree buds. Autumn colors don't prompt warning sirens. Earthly seasons don't upset us. But unexpected personal ones certainly do.

Change trampolines our lives, and when it does, God sends someone special to stabilize us. On the eve of his death, Jesus gave his followers this promise: "When the Father sends the Advocate as my representative—that is, the Holy Spirit—he will teach you everything and will remind you of everything I have told you. I am leaving you with a gift—peace of mind and heart. And the peace I give is a gift the world cannot give. So don't be troubled or afraid" (John 14:26–27 NLT).

As a departing teacher might introduce the classroom to her replacement, so Jesus introduces us to the Holy Spirit. And what a ringing endorsement he gives. Jesus calls the

Holy Spirit his "representative." The Spirit comes in the name of Christ, with equal authority and identical power. Earlier in the evening Jesus had said, "I will ask the Father, and he will give you another Counselor to be with you forever" (John 14:16 CSB).

Another Counselor. Both words shimmer. The Greek language enjoys two distinct words for *another.* One means "totally different," and the second translates "another just like the first one." When Jesus promises "another Counselor," he uses word number two, promising "another just like the first one."

The distinction is instructive. Let's say you are reading a book as you ride on a bus. Someone takes the seat next to yours, interrupts your reading, and inquires about the book. You tell him, "Max Lucado wrote it. Here, take it. I can get *another.*"

When you say, "I can get another," do you mean "another" in the sense of "any other" book? A crime novel, cookbook, or a romance paperback? Of course not. Being a person of exquisite taste, you mean a book that is identical to the one you so kindly gave away. If you had been speaking Greek, you would have used the term John used in recording Jesus' promise: *allos*—"Another one just like the first one."

And who is the first one? Jesus himself. Hence, the assurance Jesus gives to the disciples is this: "I am going away. You are entering a new season, a different chapter. Much will be different, but one thing remains constant: my presence. You will enjoy the presence of 'another Counselor.'"

Counselor means "friend" (MSG), "helper" (NKJV), "intercessor, advocate, strengthener, standby" (AMP). All descriptors attempt to portray the beautiful meaning of *parakletos*, a compound of two Greek words. *Para* means "alongside of" (think of "*para*llel" or "*para*dox"). *Kletos* means "to be called out, designated, assigned, or appointed." The Holy Spirit is designated to come alongside you. He is the presence of Jesus with and in the followers of Jesus.

Can you see how the disciples needed this encouragement? It's Thursday night before the crucifixion. By Friday's sunrise they will abandon Jesus. The breakfast hour will find them hiding in corners and crevices. At 9:00 A.M. Roman soldiers will nail Christ to a cross. By this time tomorrow he will be dead and buried. Their world is about to be flipped on its head. And Jesus wants them to know that they'll never face the future without his help.

Nor will you. You have a companion.

When you place your faith in Christ, Christ places his Spirit before, behind, and within you. Not a strange spirit, but the *same* Spirit: the *parakletos*. Everything Jesus did for his followers his Spirit does for you. Jesus taught; the Spirit teaches. Jesus healed; the Spirit heals. Jesus comforted; his Spirit comforts. As Jesus sends you into new seasons, he sends his Counselor to go with you.

God never sends you out alone. Are you on the eve of change? Heaven's message for you is clear: When everything else changes, God's presence never does.

So make friends with whatever's next.

Embrace it. Accept it. Don't resist it. Change is not only a part of life; change is a necessary part of God's strategy. To use us to change the world, he alters our assignments. Gideon: from farmer to general. God transitioned Joseph from a baby brother to an Egyptian prince. He changed David from a shepherd to a king. Peter wanted to fish the Sea of Galilee. God called him to fish for bigger things. He chose him to lead the first church. God makes holy reassignments.

But, someone might ask, what about the tragic changes God permits? Some seasons make no sense. Who can find a place in life's puzzle for the deformity of a child or the enormity of an earthquake's devastation? When a company discontinues a position or a parent is deployed . . . do such moments serve a purpose?

They do if we see them from an eternal perspective. What makes no sense in this life will make perfect sense in the next. I have proof: you in the womb.

Some prenatal features went unused before birth. You grew a nose but didn't breathe. Eyes developed, but could you see? Your tongue, toenails, and crop of hair served no function in your mother's belly. But aren't you glad you have them now?

Certain chapters in this life seem so unnecessary, like

nostrils on the preborn. Suffering. Loneliness. Disease. Holocausts. Martyrdom. Monsoons. If we assume this world exists just for pre-grave happiness, these atrocities disqualify it from doing so. But what if this earth is the womb? Might these challenges, severe as they may be, serve to prepare us, equip us for the world to come? As Paul wrote, "These little troubles are getting us ready for an eternal glory that will make all our troubles seem like nothing" (2 Cor. 4:17 CEV).

Eternal glory. I'd like a large cup, please. "One venti-sized serving of endless joy in the presence of God. Go heavy on the wonder and cut all the heartache." Go ahead and request it. The barista is still brewing. For all you know, it could be the next cup you drink.

11

The Shadow of a Doubt

"Why are you frightened?" he asked. "Why are your hearts filled with doubt?"

—Luke 24:38 NLT

There must be in God's great world a soul who has never doubted God's existence or questioned his goodness. But that soul is not writing this book.

My moments of doubt tend to surface, of all times, on Sunday mornings. I awake early, long before the family stirs, the sunrise flickers, or the paper plops on the driveway. Let the rest of the world sleep in. I don't. Sunday's my big day, the day I stand before a congregation of people who are willing to swap thirty minutes of their time for some conviction and hope.

Most weeks I have ample to go around. But occasionally I don't. (Does it bother you to know this?) Sometimes in the dawn-tinted, pre-pulpit hours, the seeming absurdity of what I believe hits me. I can remember one Easter in particular. As

I reviewed my sermon by the light of a lamp, the resurrection message felt mythic, more closely resembling an urban legend than the gospel truth. Angels perched on cemetery rocks; burial clothing needed, then not; soldiers scared stiff; a was-dead, now-walking Jesus. I half expected the Mad Hatter or the seven dwarfs to pop out of a hole at the turn of a page. A bit of a stretch, don't you think?

Sometimes I do. And when I do, I relate to the fear that God isn't. The fear that "Why?" has no answer. The fear of a pathless life. The chilling, quiet, horrifying shadows of aloneness in a valley that emerges from and leads into a fog-covered curve.

The valley of the shadow of doubt.

Perhaps you know its gray terrain? In it

- the Bible reads like Aesop's fables;
- prayers bounce back like cavern echoes;
- moral boundaries are mapped in pencil;
- believers are alternately pitied or envied; someone is deluded. But who?

To one degree or another we all venture into the valley. At one point or another we all need a plan to escape it. May I share mine? Those Sunday morning sessions of second-guessing dissipate quickly these days thanks to a small masterpiece, a wellspring of faith bubbling in the final pages of Luke's gospel. The physician-turned-historian dedicated his last chapter to answering one question: How does Christ respond when we doubt him?

Luke takes us to that upper room in Jerusalem. It's Sunday morning following Friday's crucifixion. Jesus' followers had gathered, not to change the world, but to escape it; not as gospel raconteurs, but as scared rabbits. They'd buried their hopes with the carpenter's corpse. You'd have found more courage in a chicken coop and backbone in a jellyfish. Fearless faith? Not here. Search the bearded faces of these men for a glint of resolve, a hint of courage—you'll come up empty.

One look at the bright faces of the women, however, and your heart will leap with theirs. According to Luke they exploded into the room like the sunrise, announcing a Jesus sighting.

> It was Mary Magdalene, Joanna, Mary the mother of James, and several other women who told the apostles what had happened. But the story sounded like nonsense to the men, so they didn't believe it. (Luke 24:9–11 NLT)

Periodic doubters of Christ, take note and take heart. The charter followers of Christ had doubts too. But Christ refused to leave them alone with their questions. He, as it turned out, was anything but dead and buried. When he spotted two of the disciples trudging toward a village called Emmaus, Jesus himself came up and walked along with them; but they were kept from recognizing him.

> He asked them, "What are you discussing together as you walk along?" They stood still, their faces downcast. (v. 17 NIV)

For this assignment angels wouldn't do, an emissary wouldn't suffice, an army of heaven's best soldiers wouldn't be sent. Jesus himself came to the rescue.

And how did he bolster the disciples' faith? A thousand and one tools awaited his bidding. He had marked Friday's crucifixion with an earthquake and a solar eclipse. Matthew's gospel reveals that "saints who had fallen asleep were raised; and coming out of the graves after His resurrection, they went into the holy city and appeared to many" (27:52–53). Christ could have summoned a few of them to chat with the Emmaus disciples. Or he could have toured them through the empty tomb. For that matter he could have made the rocks speak or a fig tree dance a jig. But Christ did none of these things. What did he do? "Jesus took them through the writings of Moses and all the prophets, explaining from all the Scriptures the things concerning himself" (Luke 24:27 NLT).

Well, what do you know. Christ conducted a Bible class. He led the Emmaus-bound duo through an Old Testament survey course, from the writings of Moses (Genesis through Deuteronomy) into the messages of Isaiah, Amos, and the others. He turned the Emmaus trail into a biblical timeline, pausing to describe . . . the Red Sea rumbling? Jericho tumbling?

King David stumbling? Of special import to Jesus was what the "Scriptures said about himself." His face watermarks more Old Testament stories than you might imagine. Jesus is Noah, saving humanity from disaster; Abraham, the father of a new nation; Isaac, placed on the altar by his father; Joseph, sold for a bag of silver; Moses, calling slaves to freedom; Joshua, pointing out the promised land.

Jesus "took them through the writings of Moses and all the prophets." Can you imagine Christ quoting Old Testament scripture? Did Isaiah 53 sound this way: "*I* was wounded and crushed for *your* sins. *I* was beaten that *you* might have peace" (v. 5)? Or Isaiah 28: "*I* am placing a foundation stone in Jerusalem. It is firm, a tested and precious cornerstone that is safe to build on" (v. 16)? Did he pause and give the Emmaus students a wink, saying, "I'm the stone Isaiah described"? We don't know his words, but we know their impact. The two disciples felt "our hearts burning within us while he talked" (Luke 24:32 NIV).

By now the trio had crossed northwesterly out of the rocky hills into a scented, gardened valley of olive groves and luscious fruit trees. Jerusalem's grief and bloodshed lay to their backs, forgotten in the conversation. The seven-mile hike felt more like a half-hour stroll. All too quickly fled the moments; the disciples wanted to hear more. "By this time they were nearing Emmaus and the end of their journey. Jesus acted as if he were going on, but they begged him, 'Stay the night with us.' . . . As they sat down to eat, he took the bread and blessed it. Then he broke it and gave it to them. Suddenly, their eyes were opened, and they recognized him. And at that moment he disappeared!" (vv. 28–31 NLT).

Jesus taught the Word and broke the bread, and then, like a mist on a July morning, he was gone. The Emmaus men weren't far behind. The pair dropped the broken loaf, grabbed their broken dreams, raced back to Jerusalem, and burst in on the apostles. They blurted out their discovery, only to be interrupted and upstaged by Jesus himself.

> The whole group was startled and frightened, thinking they were seeing a ghost!
>
> "Why are you frightened?" he asked. "Why are your hearts filled with doubt?" (vv. 37–38 NLT)

(Don't hurry past Christ's causal connection between fright and doubt. Unanswered qualms make for quivering disciples. No wonder Christ makes our hesitations his highest concern.)

> "Look at my hands. Look at my feet. You can see that it's really me. Touch me and make sure that I am not a ghost, because ghosts don't have bodies, as you see that I do." As he spoke, he showed them his hands and his feet.
>
> Still they stood there in disbelief, filled with joy and

> wonder. Then he asked them, "Do you have anything here to eat?" They gave him a piece of broiled fish, and he ate it as they watched.
>
> Then he said, "When I was with you before, I told you that everything written about me in the law of Moses and the prophets and in the Psalms must be fulfilled." Then he opened their minds to understand the Scriptures. (vv. 39–45 NLT)

We're detecting a pattern, aren't we?

- Jesus spots two fellows lumbering toward Emmaus, each looking as if he had just buried a best friend. Christ either catches up with or beams down to them . . . we don't know. He raises the topic of the garden of Eden and the book of Genesis. Next thing you know, a meal is eaten, their hearts are warmed, and their eyes are open.
- Jesus pays a visit to the cowardly lions of the upper room. Not a Superman-in-the-sky flyover, mind you. But a face-to-face, put-your-hand-on-my-wound visit. A meal is served, the Bible is taught, the disciples find courage, and we find two practical answers to a critical question: What would Christ have us do with our doubts?

His answer? You can be brave. Touch my body and ponder my story.

We still can, you know. We can still touch the body of Christ. We'd love to touch his physical wounds and feel the flesh of the Nazarene. Yet when we brush up against the church, we do just that. "The church is his body; it is made full and complete by Christ, who fills all things everywhere with himself" (Eph. 1:23 NLT).

Questions can make hermits out of us, driving us into hiding. Yet the cave has no answers. Christ distributes courage through community; he dissipates doubts through fellowship. He never deposits all knowledge in one person but distributes pieces of the jigsaw puzzle to many. When you interlock your understanding with mine, and we share our discoveries . . . When we mix, mingle, confess, and pray, Christ speaks.

The adhesiveness of the disciples instructs us. They stuck together. Even with ransacked hopes, they clustered in conversant community. They kept "going over all these things that had happened" (Luke 24:14 MSG). Isn't this a picture of the church—sharing notes, exchanging ideas, mulling over possibilities, lifting spirits? And as they did, Jesus showed up to teach them, proving "when two or three of you are together because of me, you can be sure that I'll be there" (Matt. 18:20 MSG).

And when he speaks, he shares his story. God's go-to therapy for doubters is his own Word. "Before you trust, you have to listen. But unless Christ's Word is preached, there's nothing to listen to" (Rom. 10:17 MSG). So listen to it.

Jack did.

Jack, an atheist, summarized the first half of his life with an incident that happened in his teenage years. He arrived at Oxford University in Oxford, England, anticipating his first glimpse of the "fabled cluster of spires and towers." Yet as he walked, he saw no sign of the great campuses. Only when he turned around did he realize he was actually walking away from the schools, headed in the wrong direction. More than thirty years later he wrote, "I did not see to what extent this little adventure was an allegory of my whole life."

He was a militant nonbeliever, devout in his resolve that God did not exist, for no God could stand for such a disaster as we call human existence. He summed up his worldview with a verse from Lucretius:

> Had God designed the world, it would not be
> A world so frail and faulty as we see.

Dismissing God, he turned his attention to academics, excelling in each field he studied. In short order the dons of Oxford took him in as a respected peer, and he began to teach and write. Yet not far beneath the surface, his doubts were taking their toll. He described his mental state with words like *abject terrorism*, *misery*, and *hopelessness*. He was angry and pessimistic, caught in a whirl of contradictions. "I maintained God did not exist. I was also angry with God for not existing."

He likely would have passed his days chugging toward the darkness, except for two factors.

A few of his close friends, also Oxford dons, rejected their materialistic view and became God-followers and Jesus-seekers. He first thought their conversion was nonsense and felt no fear of being "taken in." Then he met other faculty whom he admired, highly regarded teachers such as J. R. R. Tolkien and H. V. V. Dyson. Both men were devout believers and urged Jack to do something he'd, surprisingly, never done. Read the Bible. So he did.

As he read the New Testament, he was struck by its chief figure: Jesus Christ. Jack had dismissed Jesus as a Hebrew philosopher, a great moral teacher. But as he read, Jack began to wrestle with the claims this person made: calling himself God and offering to forgive people of their sins. Jesus was, Jack concluded, either deluded, deceptive, or the very one he claimed to be, the Son of God.

On the evening of September 19, 1931, Jack, Tolkien, and Dyson enjoyed a long walk through the beech trees and pathways of the Oxford campus—an Emmaus walk, of sorts. As they strolled, they rehashed the claims of Christ and the meaning of life. They talked late into the night. C. S. "Jack" Lewis would later recall a rush of wind that caused the first leaves to fall—a sudden breeze, which possibly came to symbolize for him the Holy Spirit. Soon after that night Lewis became a believer. He "began to know what life really is and what would have been lost by missing it." The change revolutionized his world and, consequently, the worlds of millions of readers.[1]

What caused C. S. Lewis—a gifted, brilliant, hardcore atheist—to follow Christ? Simple. He came in touch with Christ's body, his followers, and in tune with his story, the Scriptures.

Could it be this simple? Could the chasm between doubt and faith be spanned with Scripture and fellowship? Find out for yourself. Next time the shadows come, immerse yourself in the ancient stories of Moses, the prayers of David, the testimonies of the Gospels, and the epistles of Paul. Join with other seekers and make daily walks to Emmaus. And if a kind stranger joins you on the road with wise teaching . . . consider inviting him over for dinner.

12

What If Things Get Worse?

You will hear of wars and rumors of wars,
but see to it that you are not alarmed.

—Matthew 24:6 NIV

I could do without the pharmaceutical warnings. I understand their purpose, mind you. Medical manufacturers must caution against every potential tragedy so that when we take their pill and grow a third arm or turn green, we can't sue them. I get that. Still, there is something about the merger of happy faces with voice-over advisories of paralysis that just doesn't work.

Let's hope this practice of total disclosure doesn't spill over into the delivery room. It might. After all, about-to-be-born babies need to know what they are getting into. Prebirth warnings could likely become standard maternity-ward procedure. Can you imagine the scene? A lawyer stands at a woman's bedside. She's panting Lamaze breaths between contractions. He's reading the fine print of a contract in the direction of her belly.

> Welcome to the post–umbilical cord world. Be advised, however, that human life has been known, in most cases, to result in death. Some individuals have reported experiences with lethal viruses, chemical agents, and/or bloodthirsty terrorists. Birth can also result in fatal encounters with tsunamis, inebriated pilots, road rage, famine, nuclear disaster, and/or PMS. Side effects of living include superviruses, heart disease, and final exams. Human life is not recommended for anyone who cannot share a planet with evil despots or survive a flight on airplane food.

Life is a dangerous endeavor. We pass our days in the shadows of ominous realities. The power to annihilate humanity has, it seems, been placed in the hands of people who are happy to do so. Discussions of global attack prompted one small boy to beg, "Please, Mother, can't we go someplace where there isn't any sky?"[1] If the global temperature rises a few more degrees . . . if classified information falls into sinister hands . . . What if things only get worse?

Christ tells us that they will. He predicts spiritual bailouts, ecological turmoil, and worldwide persecution. Yet in the midst of it all, he contends that bravery is still an option.

> "Watch out that no one deceives you. For many will come in my name, claiming, 'I am the Messiah,' and

> will deceive many. You will hear of wars and rumors of wars, but see to it that you are not alarmed. Such things must happen, but the end is still to come. Nation will rise against nation, and kingdom against kingdom. There will be famines and earthquakes in various places. All these are the beginning of birth pains.
>
> "Then you will be handed over to be persecuted and put to death, and you will be hated by all nations because of me. At that time many will turn away from the faith and will betray and hate each other, and many false prophets will appear and deceive many people. Because of the increase of wickedness, the love of most will grow cold, but the one who stands firm to the end will be saved. And this gospel of the kingdom will be preached in the whole world as a testimony to all nations, and then the end will come." (Matt. 24:4–14 NIV)

Things are going to get bad, really bad, before they get better. And when conditions worsen, "see to it that you are not alarmed." Jesus chose a stout term for *alarmed* that he used on no other occasion. It means "to wail, to cry aloud," as if Jesus counseled the disciples, "Don't freak out when bad stuff happens."

Sitting on the Mount of Olives, in full view of the temple and the city of David, Jesus issued a "buckle your seat belt, no kidding, life can be fatal to your health" warning.

Later in the same sermon Jesus said, "False messiahs and false prophets will appear and perform great signs and wonders to deceive, if possible, even the elect" (Matt. 24:24 NIV).

Multitudes and miracles. Large audiences and spectacular deeds. Throngs of people. Displays of power. When you see them, be careful. High volume doesn't equate with sound faith. Don't be impressed by numbers or tricks. Satan can counterfeit both.

Be doctrinally diligent. Stick to one question—is this person directing listeners to Jesus? If the answer is yes, be grateful and pray for that individual. If the answer is no, get out while you still can. Along with heresy we can expect calamity. "There will be famines and earthquakes in various places. All these are the beginning of birth pains" (Matt. 24:6–8 NIV).

Nature is a pregnant creation, third-trimester heavy. When a tornado rips through a city in Oklahoma or an earthquake flattens a region in Japan, this is more than barometric changes or shifts of ancient fault lines. The universe is passing through the final hours before delivery. Painful contractions are in the forecast.

As are conflicts: "wars and rumors of wars." One nation invading another. One superpower defying another. Borders will always need checkpoints. War correspondents will always have employment. The population of the world will never see peace this side of heaven.

Christians will suffer the most. "Then you will be handed

over to be persecuted and put to death, and you will be hated by all nations because of me. At that time many will turn away from the faith and will betray and hate each other, and many false prophets will appear and deceive many people. Because of the increase of wickedness, the love of most will grow cold" (vv. 9–12 NIV).

Hatred still abounds. The Voice of the Martyrs, a Christian agency that defends religious liberties, contends that more Christ-followers have been killed for their faith in the past century than all previous centuries combined. The names of Paul, James, and Peter have been joined by Tsehay Tolessa of Ethiopia, Xu Yonghai of mainland China, Mehdi Dibaj of Iran.[2] The Global Evangelization Movement reports an average of 165,000 martyrs per year, more than four times the number of a century past.[3]

Don't freak out at the heresy, calamity, and apostasy. Don't give in or give up, for you'll soon witness the victory. "But the one who stands firm to the end will be saved. And this gospel of the kingdom will be preached in the whole world as a testimony to all nations, and then the end will come" (vv. 13–14).

Jesus equipped his followers with farsighted bravery. He listed the typhoons of life and then pointed them "to the end." Trust in ultimate victory gives ultimate bravery. Author Jim Collins makes reference to this outlook in his book *Good to Great*. Collins tells the story of Admiral James Stockdale, who was a prisoner of war for eight years during the Vietnam War.

After Stockdale's release, Collins asked him how in the world he survived eight years in a prisoner-of-war camp.

He replied, "I never lost faith in the end of the story. I never doubted not only that I would get out, but also that I would prevail in the end and turn the experience into the defining event of my life, which, in retrospect, I would not trade."

Collins then asked, "Who didn't make it out?" Admiral Stockdale replied, "Oh, that's easy. The optimists . . . they were the ones who said, 'We're going to be out by Christmas.' And Christmas would come, and Christmas would go. Then they'd say, 'We're going to be out by Easter.' And Easter would come, and Easter would go. And then Thanksgiving, and then it would be Christmas again. And they died of a broken heart."[4]

Real bravery embraces the twin realities of current difficulty and ultimate triumph. Avoid Pollyanna optimism. We gain nothing by glossing over the brutality of human existence. This is a toxic world. But neither do we join the Chicken Little chorus of gloom and doom. "The sky is falling! The sky is falling!" Somewhere between Pollyanna and Chicken Little, between blind denial and blatant panic, stands the levelheaded, clear-thinking, still-believing follower of Christ. The calmest kid on the block, not for lack of bullies, but for faith in his older Brother. The old people of God knew this peace: "Though a host encamp against me, my heart shall not fear; though war arise against me, yet I will be confident" (Ps. 27:3 RSV).

Christ says to us, "See to it that you are not alarmed" (Matt. 24:6 NIV).

"Keep your head and don't panic" (MSG).

"See that you are not troubled" (NKJV).

Remember: "All these [challenging times] are the beginning of sorrows" (Matt. 24:8 NIV), and birth pangs aren't all bad. (Easy for me to say.) Birth pains signal the onset of the final push. The obstetrician assures the mom-to-be, "It's going to hurt for a time, but it's going to get better." Jesus assures us of the same. Global conflicts indicate our date on the maternity calendar. We are in the final hours, just a few pushes from delivery, a few brief ticks of eternity's clock from the great crowning of creation. A whole new world is coming!

All things, big and small, flow out of the purpose of God and serve his good will. When the world appears out of control, it isn't. When warmongers appear to be in charge, they aren't. When ecological catastrophes dominate the day, don't let them dominate you.

Let's trust our heavenly Father in the manner Peter Wirth trusted his earthly one.

Peter was a twenty-one-year-old university student when he began to experience severe pain in his right shoulder. He called his father for advice. Most students would do the same: call home for counsel. But few students have a better parent to call in such a situation. Peter's father, Michael, is a world-renowned orthopedic surgeon who specializes in shoulders.

Peter calling Dr. Wirth with a shoulder problem is like Bill Gates's daughter calling him with a software question.

Michael initially attributed Peter's pain to weight lifting. But after numbness and tingling set in, the doctor grew suspicious of an extremely rare shoulder condition called deep vein thrombosis. A clot was forming in his son's shoulder, dangerously close to his heart. Michael was not only acquainted with the condition; he had coauthored the paper on how to treat it. He sent Peter to the emergency room and told him to request an ultrasound. Turns out, Michael's long-distance diagnosis was right on target. Peter was immediately admitted to the hospital, where the clot was dissolved and his earthly life was extended.

Wouldn't it be great to have such a father?

We do. He has diagnosed the pain of the world and written the book on its treatment. We can trust him. As someone has said, "Everything will work out in the end. If it's not working out, it's not the end."

13

The One Healthy Terror

They fell on their faces and were greatly afraid. But Jesus came and touched them and said, "Arise, and do not be afraid."

—Matthew 17:6–7

A woman in the hotel check-in line was holding one of my books under her arm. I was hesitant to introduce myself lest she explain that her doctor had prescribed the volume as insomnia treatment. But I took the risk. She actually said she liked it. But on second glance she didn't believe that I was who I claimed to be.

She flipped open the dust jacket, looked at my picture, then up at me. "You're not Max Lucado."

"Yes, I am. The picture on the book was taken many years ago; I've changed."

With no smile she looked again at the photo. "No," she

insisted, "Max Lucado has a mustache, no wrinkles, and a full head of hair."

"He used to," I explained.

She wouldn't budge. "He still does."

I started to show her my driver's license but opted to let her live with her delusion. After all, if she wanted to remember me as a thirty-year-old, who was I to argue?

Besides, I understand her reluctance. Once you have someone pegged, it's easier to leave him there. She had me figured out. Defined. Captured. Freeze-framed in a two-by-three image. Max-in-a-box.

Boxes bring wonderful order to our world. They keep cereal from spilling and books from tumbling. When it comes to containing stuff, boxes are masterful. But when it comes to explaining people, they fall short. And when it comes to defining Christ, no box works.

His Palestinian contemporaries tried, mind you. They designed an assortment of boxes. But he never fit one. They called him a revolutionary; then he paid his taxes. They labeled him as a country carpenter, but he confounded scholars. They came to see his miracles, but he refused to cater. He defied easy definitions. He was a Jew who attracted Gentiles. A rabbi who gave up on synagogues. A holy man who hung out with streetwalkers and turncoats. In a male-dominated society, he recruited women. In an anti-Roman culture, he opted not to denounce Rome. He talked like a king, yet lived like a pilgrim. People tried to designate him. They couldn't.

We still try.

My taxi-driving friend in Brazil kept a miniature Jesus superglued to his car dashboard. Anytime he needed a parking place or green light, he rubbed his plastic do-me-a-favor Jesus.

The preacher occupying the midnight broadcast time slot assured me and other late-night cable viewers that prosperity was only a prayer away. Just ask the make-me-a-buck Jesus.

I once reduced Christ down to a handful of doctrines. He was a recipe, and I had the ingredients. Mix them correctly, and the Jesus-of-my-making would appear.

Politicians pull box-sized versions of Jesus off the shelf, asserting that Jesus would most certainly vote green, conservative; often, never; like a hawk, dove, or eagle. The Jesus-of-my-politics comes in handy during elections.

Box-sized gods. You'll find them in the tight grip of people who prefer a god they can manage, control, and predict. This topsy-turvy life requires a tame deity, doesn't it? In a world out of control, we need a god we can control, a comforting presence akin to a lapdog or the kitchen cat. We call and he comes. We pet and he purrs. *If we can just keep God in his place . . .*

Peter, James, and John must have tried. How else can you explain this box-blowing expedition on which Jesus took them?

> Now after six days Jesus took Peter, James, and John his brother, led them up on a high mountain by themselves; and He was transfigured before them. His face shone like the sun, and His clothes became as white as the light. And behold, Moses and Elijah appeared to them, talking with Him. Then Peter answered and said to Jesus, "Lord, it is good for us to be here; if You wish, let us make here three tabernacles: one for You, one for Moses, and one for Elijah."
>
> While he was still speaking, behold, a bright cloud overshadowed them; and suddenly a voice came out of the cloud, saying, "This is My beloved Son, in whom I am well pleased. Hear Him!" And when the disciples heard it, they fell on their faces and were greatly afraid. But Jesus came and touched them and said, "Arise, and do not be afraid." When they had lifted up their eyes, they saw no one but Jesus only. (Matt. 17:1–8)

The high points of Scripture seem to occur on the high points of earth. Abraham offering Isaac on Mount Moriah. Moses witnessing the burning bush on Mount Sinai. Elijah ascending to heaven from Horeb. Christ redeeming humanity on a hill called Calvary. And Jesus peeling back his epidermis on Mount Hermon.

No one knows for sure, but most historians place this event on a 9,200-foot-tall mountain called Mount Hermon. It towers over the northern Israeli landscape, visible from the Dead Sea a hundred miles away. This gigantic, snowy peak was the perfect place for Christ to retreat with Peter, James, and John. Away from the clamoring crowds and nagging controversies, Jesus could have the undivided attention of his three closest friends.

Together they could look out over the turquoise-colored Sea of Galilee or the great plain, lumpy with vine-clad hills. Here they could pray. "He [Jesus] took Peter, John, and James and went up on the mountain to pray" (Luke 9:28). Christ needed strength. He was only months from the cross. The spikes of the soldiers and the spite of the crowd loomed ahead. He needed fortitude to face them, and he wanted his followers to see where he got it.

At some point while praying, the gentle carpenter who ate matzos and shish kebabs and spoke with a Galilean accent erupted into a cosmic figure of light. "He was transfigured before them. His face shone like the sun, and His clothes became as white as the light" (Matt. 17:2).

Light spilled out of him. Brilliant. Explosive. Shocking. Brightness poured through every pore of his skin and stitch of his robe. Jesus on fire. To look at his face was to look squarely into Alpha Centauri. Mark wants us to know that Jesus' "clothes shimmered, glistening white, whiter than any bleach could make them" (Mark 9:3 MSG).

This radiance was not the work of a laundry; it was the presence of God. Scripture habitually equates God with light and light with holiness. "God is light; in him there is no darkness at all" (1 John 1:5 NIV). The transfigured Christ, then, is Christ in his purest form.

It's also Christ as his truest self, wearing his pre-Bethlehem and post-resurrection wardrobe. One "who is holy, blameless, pure, set apart from sinners" (Heb. 7:26 NIV). A diamond with no flaw, a rose with no bruise, a song on perfect pitch, and a poem with impeccable rhyme.

In a flash Peter, James, and John were mosquitoes in an eagle's shadow. They'd never seen Jesus in such a fashion. Walk on water, multiply bread, talk to the wind, banish demons, and raise the dead, yes. But a standing torch? Turns out, Jesus was just getting warmed up.

Two visitors appeared: Moses and Elijah, the Washington and Lincoln of the Jewish people. Their portraits hung in the entryway to the Hebrew Hall of Fame. And here they stood, the answer to Jesus' prayer. Don't we half expect Peter, James, and John to repeat their Sea of Galilee question: "What kind of man is this?" (Matt. 8:27 NIV)?

About this point Peter cleared his throat to speak. Fire on the mountain became foot in the mouth. "Lord, it is good for us to be here; if You wish, let us make here three tabernacles: one for You, one for Moses, and one for Elijah" (Matt. 17:4).

These words might seem harmless to us, even a good idea to some. Not from God's perspective. Peter's idea of three tabernacles was so off base and inappropriate that God wouldn't permit him to finish the sentence. "While he [Peter] was still speaking, behold, a bright cloud overshadowed them; and suddenly a voice came out of the cloud, saying, 'This is My beloved Son, in whom I am well pleased. Hear Him!'" (v. 5).

Beloved means "priceless" and "unique." There is none other like Christ. Not Moses. Not Elijah. Not Peter. Not Zoroaster, Buddha, or Muhammad. No one in heaven or on earth. Jesus, the Father declared, is not "a son" or even "the best of all sons." He is the "beloved Son."

Peter missed this. He placed Christ in a respectable box labeled "great men of history." He wanted to give Jesus *and* Moses *and* Elijah equal honor. God would have none of it. Christ has no counterparts.

Peter, James, and John didn't speak anymore. They saw what no other people have seen: Christ in cosmic greatness. Words don't work in such a moment. Blood drained from their faces. Skin ashened. Knees wobbled and pulses raced. "They fell on their faces and were greatly afraid" (v. 6).

Fire on the mountain led to fear on the mountain. A holy, healthy fear. They were gripped deep in their gut that God was, at once, everywhere and here. The very sight of the glowing Galilean sucked all air and arrogance out of them, leaving them appropriately prostrate. "They fell on their faces and were greatly afraid."

This is the fear of the Lord. Most of our fears are poisonous. They steal sleep and pillage peace. But this fear is different.

"From a biblical perspective, there is nothing neurotic about fearing God. The neurotic thing is *not* to be afraid, or to be afraid of the wrong thing. That is why God chooses to be known to us, so that we may stop being afraid of the wrong thing. When God is fully revealed to us and we 'get it,' then we experience the conversion of our fear. . . . 'Fear of the Lord' is the deeply sane recognition that we are not God."[1]

How long since you felt this fear? Since a fresh understanding of Christ buckled your knees and emptied your lungs? Since a glimpse of him left you speechless and breathless? If it's been a while, that explains your fears.

When Christ is great, our fears are not.

As awe of Jesus expands, fears of life diminish. A big God translates into big bravery. A small view of God generates no bravery.

This must be why Jesus took the disciples up the mountain. He saw the box in which they had confined him. He saw the future that awaited them: the fireside denial of Peter, prisons of Jerusalem and Rome, the demands of the church, and the persecutions of Nero. A box-sized version of God simply would not work. So Jesus blew the sides out of their preconceptions.

May he blow the sides out of ours.

Don't we need to know the transfigured Christ? One who spits holy fires? Who convenes and commands historical figures? Who occupies the loftiest perch and wears the only true crown of the universe, God's beloved Son? One who takes friends to Mount Hermon's peak so they can peek into heaven?

Ascend it. Stare long and longingly at the Bonfire, the Holy One, the Highest One, the Only One. As you do, all your fears, save the fear of Christ himself, will melt like ice cubes on a summer sidewalk. You will agree with David: "The LORD is my light and my salvation; whom shall I fear?" (Ps. 27:1).

The longer we live in Christ, the greater he becomes in us. It's not that he changes but that we do; we see more of him. We see dimensions, aspects, and characteristics we never saw before, increasing and astonishing increments of his purity, power, and uniqueness. Define Jesus with a doctrine or confine him to an opinion? By no means. We'll sooner capture the Caribbean in a butterfly net than we'll capture Christ in a box.

In the end we respond like the apostles. We, too, fall on our faces and worship. And when we do, the hand of the carpenter extends through the tongue of towering fire and touches us. "Arise, and do not be afraid" (Matt. 17:7).

Here's my hunch. Peter, James, and John descended the mountain sunburned and smiling, with a spring in their step, if not a slight swagger. With a Messiah like this one, who could hurt them?

Here's my other hunch. Mount Hermon's still ablaze and has space for guests.

14

Conclusion

William's Psalm

At 8:17 on the evening of March 3, 1943, bomb-raid sirens bansheed through the air above London, England. Workers and shoppers stopped on sidewalks and boulevards and searched the skies. Buses came to a halt and emptied their passengers. Drivers screeched their brakes and stepped out of their cars. Gunfire could be heard in the distance. Nearby anti-aircraft artillery forces launched a salvo of rockets. Throngs on the streets began to scream. Some people threw themselves onto the ground. Others covered their heads and shouted, "They are starting to drop them!" Everyone looked above for enemy planes. The fact that they saw none did nothing to dampen their hysteria.

People raced toward the Bethnal Green Underground

Station, where more than five hundred citizens had already taken refuge. In the next ten minutes fifteen hundred more would join them.

Trouble began when a rush of safety seekers reached the stairwell entrance at the same time. A woman carrying a baby lost her footing on one of the nineteen uneven steps leading down from the street. Her stumble interrupted the oncoming flow, causing a domino of others to tumble on top of her. Within seconds, hundreds of horrified people were thrown together, piling up like laundry in a basket. Matters worsened when the late arrivers thought they were being deliberately blocked from entering (they weren't). So they began to push. The chaos lasted for less than a quarter of an hour. The disentangling of bodies took until midnight. In the end 173 men, women, and children died.

No bombs had been dropped.

Fusillades didn't kill the people. Fear did.[1]

Fear loves a good stampede. Fear's payday is blind panic, unfounded disquiet, and sleepless nights. Fear's been making a good living lately.

Here's a test. How far do you have to go to hear the reminder "Be afraid"? How near is your next "You are in trouble" memo? A glance at the internet update on the phone, computer, or television screen? According to the media the world is one scary place.

And we suspect a campaign to keep it that way. Fear sells.

Fear glues watchers to their seats, sells magazines off the racks, and puts money in the pockets of the system. Newscasts have learned to rely on a glossary of trouble-stirring phrases to keep our attention: "Coming up, the frightening truth about sitting in traffic." "How chocolate affects your IQ." "What you may not know about the water you drink."

We are peppered with bad news. Global warming, asteroid attack, pandemics, genocide, wars, earthquakes, hurricanes, HIV... Does it ever stop? The bad news is taking its toll. We are the most worried culture that has ever lived. For the first time since the end of the Second World War, parents expect that life for the next generation will be worse than it was for them.[2]

There's a stampede of fear out there. Let's not get caught in it. Let's be among those who stay calm. Let's recognize danger but not be overwhelmed. Acknowledge threats but refuse to be defined by them. Let others breathe the polluted air of anxiety, not us. Let's be numbered among those who hear a different voice—God's. Enough of these shouts of despair, wails of doom. Why pay heed to the doomsdayer on Wall Street or the purveyor of gloom in the media? We will turn to our Maker, and because we do, we will fear less.

Bravery does not panic; it prays. Bravery does not bemoan; it believes. Bravery does not languish; it listens. It listens to the voice of God calling through Scripture, "Fear not!" It hears Christ's voice comforting through the hospital corridors, graveyards, and war zones:

> "Be of good cheer! It is I; do not be afraid." (Matt. 14:27)
>
> "When reports come in of wars and rumored wars, keep your head and don't panic." (Matt. 24:6 MSG)
>
> "Let not your heart be troubled." (John 14:1)
>
> "Do not fear therefore; you are of more value than many sparrows." (Luke 12:7)

We will follow the astounding example of William Fariss, who, as a seven-year-old boy, watched his house go up in flames. He is the son of Pioneer Bible translators in West Africa, a bright young man with a voracious interest in dinosaurs and animals. His family lived in a tin-roofed house covered by a layer of thatch. One day the wind lifted sparks from a nearby fire, and they exploded the Farisses' thatch roof in flames. The family attempted to save the house but stood no chance in the dry air and hot African sun. As they witnessed the fire reduce their home to cinders and charred brick, William's mother heard him praying. She noted that the words were psalm-like, and when she heard him repeat it a few days later, she wrote down what he said.

> Through wind and rain
> Through fire and lava
> The Lord will never leave you.
> Through earthquakes and floods

Through changing sea levels and burning ash
The Lord will never leave you.
If you love Him, He will bless you
and He will give you many things.

Who can stop the Lord?
Who can chase a cheetah across the plains
of Africa?
The Lord, He can.
Who can stand on Mount Everest?
Who can face a rhinoceros?
The Lord.
The Lord can give you sheep and goats
and cows and ducks and chickens
and dogs and cats.
The Lord can give you anything He wants to.

Who can stop the Lord?
Who can face an elephant?
Who is brave enough to face a lion?
The Lord.
Who's as fast as a horse?
Who can catch a blue whale?
Who is brave enough to face a giant squid?
The Lord.
Just as Jesus died on the cross,

so the Lord has done so.
The Lord will never leave His people.
The Bible is His word.
The Lord is a good leader.

The Lord who loves you.
And He will not forsake His people.
The end.[3]

Though the flames threatened, the boy saw God in the flames. William trusted God and feared less. So can we.

Amen, William. And amen.

Discussion Guide

Chapter 1: Why Are You Afraid?

1. "Envision a day, just one day, absent the dread of failure, rejection, and calamity. Can you imagine a life with no fear?" How would your life be different today if all fear were erased from your heart?
2. "The fear-filled cannot love deeply. Love is risky. They cannot give to the poor. Benevolence has no guarantee of return. The fear-filled cannot dream wildly. What if their dreams sputter and fall from the sky? The worship of safety emasculates greatness."

   Why does fear make it harder to love? Why does fear make it hard to give generously? How does fear stifle our dreams?
3. Read Matthew 8:23–27. What connection does Jesus make between fear and faith in verse 26?
4. For one whole week meditate on 2 Timothy 1:7 in the translation of your choice. Repeat the verse in your head as often as you can.

Chapter 2: God's Ticked Off at Me

1. "Memories of dropped passes fade slowly. They stir a lonely fear, a fear that we have disappointed people, that we have let

down the team, that we've come up short. A fear that, when needed, we didn't do our part, that others suffered from our fumbles and bumbles."

What do you typically do when such thoughts hit you? Do you dwell on them? Stew over them? Pray about them? Try to forget them?

2. "Might bravery begin when the problem of sin is solved?"

   Why would bravery begin with the solving of the problem of sin? What often fuels a lack of bravery?
3. Read John 3:16–18, 36. Why did God send his Son into the world? What was *not* the Son's purpose?
4. Examine the Scripture stories of these characters who disappointed God: Peter (Mark 14:27–31; John 21:15–19); David (2 Sam. 11); the Samaritan woman (John 4:1–42). How do their stories give you hope when you disappoint God?

Chapter 3: Woe, Be Gone

1. "Shortfalls and depletions inhabit our trails. Not enough time, luck, credit, wisdom, intelligence. We are running out of everything, it seems, and so we worry. But worry doesn't work." What are you running out of that prompts you to worry?
2. "Standing next to the disciples was the solution to their problems . . . but they didn't go to him. They stopped their count at seven and worried."

   Why do you suppose we don't immediately turn to Jesus when faced with a shortage of some kind?
3. Read Matthew 6:25–34. What reasons for not worrying does Jesus give in this passage?

4. If you want to battle your fear of lack and instead enjoy a deep sense of *peaceful*ness, then for at least one week try the following regimen:

    Pray, first (1 Peter 5:7).

    Easy, now (Ps. 37:7).

    Act on it (Matt. 25:14–28).

    Compile a worry list (Luke 10:41).

    Evaluate your worry categories (Matt. 6:25–27).

    Focus on today (Matt. 6:34; Heb. 4:16).

    Unleash a worry army (1 Thess. 5:25).

    Let God be enough (Matt. 6:28–33).

Chapter 4: My Child Is in Danger

1. "Jesus heeds the concern in the parent's heart."

    In what areas of dealing with your children do you most need Jesus' help right now?
2. "Horror called from one side. Hope compelled from the other. Tragedy, then trust. Jairus heard two voices and had to choose which one he would heed. Don't we all?"

    How can you train yourself to listen consistently to the voice of Jesus rather than to other voices that call you to fear?
3. Read Luke 8:40–56. How does this passage show that a delay in receiving an answer to a desperate prayer does not necessarily mean a no?
4. Pick at least two of the following promises from Scripture and memorize them, repeating them to yourself every day for a month. Note what this does to your level of fear regarding your

children. Passages: Deuteronomy 4:40; 5:29; 30:19; Psalm 37:25; Proverbs 20:7; Acts 2:38–39.

Chapter 5: I'm Sinking Fast

1. "It is in storms that he does his finest work, for it is in storms that he has our keenest attention."

   Describe how you have seen Jesus in a storm.

2. "We aren't to be oblivious to the overwhelming challenges that life brings. We're to counterbalance them with long looks at God's accomplishments. . . . Do whatever it takes to keep your gaze on Jesus."

   Describe some of God's greatest accomplishments in your life during the past year.

3. Read Romans 8:35–39. How can we become victorious, "more than conquerors," even when facing overwhelming circumstances?
4. Choose one action to take this week to help arm you in the battle against fear.

   Memorize scripture.

   Ponder the testimonies of faithful Christians.

Chapter 6: There's a Dragon in My Closet

1. "What's your worst fear? A fear of public failure, unemployment, or heights? The fear that you'll never find the right spouse or enjoy good health? The fear of being trapped, abandoned, or forgotten?"

   Answer the question above. Describe your physical and emotional response to this fear.

2. "How many people spend life on the edge of the pool? Consulting caution. Ignoring faith. Never taking the plunge. . . . For fear of the worst, they never enjoy life at its best."

   Name one area of life in which you would like to take the plunge.
3. Read Mark 14:32–42. What was the worst-case scenario facing Christ? What made him so troubled and distressed? How did he respond to it?
4. Although it will be uncomfortable, pull back the curtains and expose your fears, each and every one. When you examine them in the sunlight, what happens?

Chapter 7: This Brutal Planet

1. "Contrary to what we'd hope, good people aren't exempt from violence."

   Why do you think good people have no exemption from violence?
2. "Satan cannot reach you without passing through him [God]."

   Does it comfort you to know that Satan cannot reach you without passing through God? Explain.
3. Read Hebrews 11:35–40. What kind of violence was directed against people of faith as described in this passage?
4. Jesus himself suffered tremendously at the hands of violent men. Memorize Hebrews 12:2–3. How did Jesus endure the cross? Take some extended time to meditate on what he did so that you won't become weary or discouraged in your own walk of faith.

Chapter 8: Make-Believe Money

1. "The resounding and recurring message of Scripture is clear: God owns it all. God shares it all. Trust him, not stuff!"

   When can you tell that you've started to trust money more than God? What are some telltale signs?
2. Why does trusting in money always lead to a dystopia of unhappiness?
3. Read Luke 12:16–21. What does it mean to be rich toward God? Do you have this kind of riches? Explain.
4. Regardless of your financial position, this week give generously—more than you can really afford—to some group or individual who advances the cause of Christ. Write in a journal how your giving affects you and your household.

Chapter 9: Scared to Death

1. "Jesus elevates funerals to the same hope level as weddings. From his perspective the trip to the cemetery and the walk down the aisle warrant identical excitement."

   Why should funerals give Christians as much hope as weddings?

   Can you say you are excited about your own death? Explain.
2. "Let's allow the resurrection to sink into the fibers of our hearts and define the way we look at the grave."

   How does one's attitude toward death reveal what he or she truly believes about the resurrection?

What are some practical ways you can let the reality of the resurrection sink into the fibers of your heart?

3. Read Hebrews 2:14–15. Who had the power of death? How did Jesus destroy both him and his power?

   How can we be released from a fear of death? In what way is this fear a kind of bondage?

4. What difference does a vibrant faith in Christ make when death comes calling?

Chapter 10: Caffeinated Life

1. "If only we could order life the way we order gourmet coffee. Wouldn't you love to mix and match the ingredients of your future?"

   If you could mix and match the ingredients of your future, what would your future look like?

2. "Change is not only a part of life; change is a necessary part of God's strategy. To use us to change the world, he alters our assignments."

   How has God altered your assignment? How might he be altering it right now?

3. Read John 14:16–18, 26–27. What promises does Jesus give us in verses 16–18? How can these promises help us battle the fear of what's next?

   What is the vital connection between verses 26 and 27? How is the Spirit working in your life?

4. List the major fears you've had in the past five years. How many actually came to pass? What did you waste while worrying over nothing?

Chapter 11: The Shadow of a Doubt

1. "Periodic doubters of Christ, take note and take heart. The charter followers of Christ had doubts too. But Christ refused to leave them alone with their questions."

   Under what circumstances are you most likely to become a periodic doubter of Christ?

2. "Christ distributes courage through community; he dissipates doubts through fellowship. He never deposits all knowledge in one person but distributes pieces of the jigsaw puzzle to many."

   How does Christ distribute courage through community and dissipate doubts through fellowship?

   Are you active in a local church? In what ways do you serve and receive help there?

3. Read Romans 10:17. How does faith come, according to this passage?

   What does this imply about regular Bible reading and study?

4. "Next time the shadows come, immerse yourself in the ancient stories of Moses, the prayers of David, the testimonies of the Gospels, and the epistles of Paul. Join with other seekers and make daily walks to Emmaus."

   This week, immerse yourself in the great stories of the Bible that showcase God's power and love.

Chapter 12: What If Things Get Worse?

1. "[It was] as if Jesus counseled the disciples, 'Don't freak out when bad stuff happens.'"

Do you have a personal action plan for dealing with bad stuff? Explain.

2. "All things, big and small, flow out of the purpose of God and serve his good will. When the world appears out of control, it isn't."

   How can bad stuff serve God's good will? Describe a time in your life when bad stuff served God's good will.

   How do you generally react when your world seems to be spinning out of control? How would you counsel yourself in such times?

3. Read Psalm 46:1–11. What kind of fears do verses 2–3 and 6 mention? How does the psalmist counteract these fears?

   How do verses 8–11 allay our fears of major catastrophes?

4. Write out the following statement and place it in a prominent location that you will see often (on your refrigerator, in your car, on your office desk, etc.): "Everything will work out in the end. If it's not working out, it's not the end."

Chapter 13: The One Healthy Terror

1. "When it comes to defining Christ, no box works."

   Into what boxes have you tried to put Christ?

   Why is it impossible to put Jesus Christ into a box?

2. "Fire on the mountain led to fear on the mountain. A holy, healthy fear."

   How can a true reverence of God give you stability in times of uncertainty and fear?

3. Read Matthew 17:1–8. Why do you suppose Jesus wanted his

three closest disciples to see him transfigured just before his death?

4. Carefully study and compare the four major accounts of the transfiguration of Christ found in the Bible: Matthew 17:1–8; Mark 9:2–8; Luke 9:28–36; 2 Peter 1:16–18. Make a list of the story elements you find there. Then take time to ponder not only the event of the transfiguration but how it affected Peter, James, and John.

Chapter 14: Conclusion

1. "Fear loves a good stampede."

   In what way is fear contagious?

   How can you avoid joining the stampede?

2. "Let's be among those who stay calm. Let's recognize danger but not be overwhelmed. Acknowledge threats but refuse to be defined by them."

   Describe some ways you can recognize danger but not be overwhelmed by it.

3. Read Isaiah 8:12–14. Against what fears did Isaiah caution his countrymen?

   What fear were they to cultivate? How would this righteous fear help them in the here and now?

4. For one week meditate several times a day on a single verse of Scripture from God's own mouth: "I will never leave you nor forsake you" (Heb. 13:5). At the end of each day, spend at least ten minutes praising him for his eternal commitment to you.

Notes

Chapter 1: Why Are You Afraid?

1. Shelley Wachsmann, *The Sea of Galilee Boat: An Extraordinary 2000 Year Old Discovery* (New York: Plenum Press, 1995), 326–28.

Chapter 2: God's Ticked Off at Me

1. Ken Rodriguez, "History Keeps Digging Its Horns into Texas Receiver," *San Antonio Express-News*, October 26, 2001.

Chapter 5: I'm Sinking Fast

1. Wachsmann, *The Sea of Galilee Boat*, 39, 121.

Chapter 6: There's a Dragon in My Closet

1. Joshua Piven and David Borgenicht, *The Complete Worst-Case Scenario Survival Handbook* (San Francisco: Chronicle Books, 2007).
2. Pierre Benoit, quoted in Frederick Dale Bruner, *Matthew: A Commentary*, vol. 2, *The Churchbook: Matthew 13–28* (Dallas: Word Publishing, 1990), 979.
3. Bruner, *Matthew*, 978.

Chapter 7: This Brutal Planet

1. Peggy Nelson, conversation with author. Used by permission.
2. Charles Colson, *Loving God* (Grand Rapids: Zondervan, 1983), 27–34.

3. Aleksandr Solzhenitsyn, *The Gulag Archipelago, 1918–1956: An Experiment in Literary Investigation*, trans. Thomas P. Whitney (New York: HarperPerennial, 2007), 309–12.

Chapter 8: Make-Believe Money

1. Walter Brueggemann, "The Liturgy of Abundance, the Myth of Scarcity," *The Christian Century* 116, no. 10 (March 24, 1999), www.christiancentury.org/article/2012-01/liturgy-abundance-myth-scarcity.
2. Anup Shah, "Poverty Facts and Stats," Global Issues, last updated January 7, 2013, www.globalissues.org/article/26/poverty-facts-and-stats.

Chapter 9: Scared to Death

1. Donald G. Bloesch, *The Last Things: Resurrection, Judgment, Glory* (Downers Grove, IL: InterVarsity Press, 2004), 125.
2. Bloesch, *Last Things*, 125.
3. John Blanchard, *Whatever Happened to Hell?* (Wheaton, IL: Crossway Books, 1995), 63.
4. Blanchard, *Whatever Happened to Hell?*, 62.
5. N. T. Wright, *Christian Origins and the Question of God*, vol. 3, The Resurrection of the Son of God (Minneapolis: Fortress Press, 2003), 205–6.

Chapter 11: The Shadow of a Doubt

1. Armand M. Nicholi Jr., *The Question of God: C. S. Lewis and Sigmund Freud Debate God, Love, Sex, and the Meaning of Life* (New York: Free Press, 2002), 84–92, 111–14.

Chapter 12: What If Things Get Worse?

1. Joanna Bourke, *Fear: A Cultural History* (Emeryville, CA: Shoemaker and Hoard, 2005), 195.
2. DC Talk and the Voice of the Martyrs, *Jesus Freaks* (Tulsa, OK: Albury Publishing, 1999), 133, 167, 208.
3. "Status of Global Mission, 2001, in Context of 20th and 21st Centuries," Global Evangelization Movement, Worldwide Persian Outreach, www.farsinet.com/pwo/world_mission.html.
4. Jim Collins, *Good to Great: Why Some Companies Make the Leap . . . and Others Don't* (New York: HarperCollins, 2001), 83–85.

Chapter 13: The One Healthy Terror

1. Ellen F. Davis, *Getting Involved with God: Rediscovering the Old Testament* (Cambridge, MA: Cowley Press, 2001), 102–3.

Chapter 14: Conclusion

1. Bourke, *Fear,* 232–33.
2. Frank Furedi, *Culture of Fear Revisited: Risk-Taking and the Morality of Low Expectation,* 4th ed. (New York: Continuum Books, 2006), 68.
3. Greg Pruett, "President's Blog," Pioneer Bible Translators, February 27, 2008, http://www.pioneerbible.org/cms/tiki-view _blog_post.php?blogld=2&postld=9.

Inspired by what you just read?

Connect with Max

UPWORDS

The nonprofit teaching ministry of Max Lucado

Listen to Max's teaching ministry, UpWords, on the radio and online. Visit MaxLucado.com for more resources for spiritual growth and encouragement, including:

- Archives of UpWords, Max's daily radio program, and a list of radio stations where it airs
- Daily devotionals and emails from Max
- *The Max Lucado Encouraging Word Podcast*
- *Fresh Hope* YouTube Teaching Show
- Video teaching and articles
- Online store with information on new books and special offers

1-800-822-9673
UpWords Ministries
P.O. Box 692170
San Antonio, TX 78269-2170
info@maxlucado.com

MaxLucado.com

Join the Max Lucado community:
Facebook.com/MaxLucado
Instagram.com/MaxLucado
X.com/MaxLucado
YouTube.com/MaxLucadoOfficial